MW01698150

Great Things He Hath Done

A Legacy of Commitment and Growth

(ABWE 1927–2000)

Great Things He Hath Done

A Legacy of Commitment and Growth

(ABWE 1927–2000)

Compiled by Jay Walsh

Association of Baptists for World Evangelism
P.O. Box 8585
Harrisburg, PA 17105-8585
(717) 774-7000

ABWE Canada
160 Adelaide St. South, Suite 205
London, Ontario N5Z 3L1
CANADA
(519) 690-1009

ABWE PUBLISHING®

GREAT THINGS HE HATH DONE

Harrisburg, Pennsylvania 17105

Library of Congress cataloging-in-publication data (application pending)

Walsh, D. Jay, 1932–

Compiled from *Heritage & Harvest* © 1981 (ABWE's first 53 years) and *Valued Heritage and Veritable Harvest* © 1990 (ABWE during the 1980's)

Great Things He Hath Done: A Legacy of Commitment and Growth (ABWE from 1927 to 2000)

Missions—History—Non-Fiction
ISBN: 1-888796-20-0

Printed in the United States of America.

TABLE OF CONTENTS

DEDICATION

This book is lovingly dedicated to Dr. Joseph M. Stowell, who was elected to the ABWE Advisory Council on June 14, 1940, and to the full board and Executive Committee on May 18, 1950.

He became vice-president of ABWE on June 9, 1955, an office he held until January 1986. During this time, he also served as a representative of ABWE.

For your 60 years with the mission, the entire ABWE family salutes you.

Dr. Joseph Stowell

FOREWORD

A faithful Baptist pastor, Dr. John Powell, once stated, "Baptists are so busy making history they do not take time to write it." This is a sobering indictment. Israel was reminded of the need to remember and record the past. In Psalm 145:4–12 we read,

"One generation shall praise thy works to another, and shall declare thy mighty acts . . . to make known to the sons of men . . . the glorious majesty of His kingdom."

This mission agency is dedicated to remembering and recording God's awesome acts. We desire to follow the psalmist's instructions:

"They shall abundantly utter the memory of thy great goodness" (Psalm 145:7).

Veteran missionary to Bangladesh, Jay Walsh, has undertaken the task of compiling ABWE's history from 1927 to 2000. To accomplish this, he condensed the earlier works of *Heritage & Harvest,* written by ABWE's president emeritus, Harold Commons, and *Valued Heritage and Veritable Harvest,* written by ABWE's administrative consultant and enlistment director for nearly a quarter-century, Harold Amstutz. Jay then researched ABWE's progress in the 1990's.

In reading the following pages, you will be able to see how God has moved in mysterious ways to reap a rich harvest through ABWE worldwide. The image you will see over and over again is that of faithful missionaries expediting their major responsibility of winning people to Christ, discipling them in the Word of God, and planting churches. The book will guide you through the history of a mission agency that has sought to be true to the Word of God, and give Him all the glory and honor.

Wendell Kempton, President
Association of Baptists for World Evangelism
December 1999

PREFACE

My purpose in writing *Great Things He Hath Done* was not to try to improve on the works of Dr. Harold T. Commons and Dr. Harold Amstutz in their earlier volumes, but to capture ABWE's history from 1927 to 2000 in a single, abbreviated volume. To accomplish this goal, it was necessary to condense the earlier books and add historical research from the last decade of the 1900's.

Readers will notice the change in writing style from Harold Commons to Harold Amstutz to Jay Walsh. However, we shared a common goal: to paint with broad brush strokes ABWE's contribution to world evangelism and church planting in the twentieth century.

In a technical book such as this, with so many people working in so many areas of ABWE's worldwide ministries, it was necessary and prudent that those most involved with the ministry be given the opportunity to read the material and make suggestions. Their input has greatly improved the final product. Their doing so placed greater responsibility on the ABWE Publications Department.

I am deeply indebted to my friend and colleague Jeannie Lockerbie Stephenson for her editorial work and for the UPDATES 2000, which bring into current perspective the countries where ABWE works today. Becky Davey, Kristen Stagg (assistant editor), and Wally Stephenson, also gave their time and effort. Thanks to all of them for their important part in making this book a reality.

David Jay Walsh
February 2000

One

In the Beginning

In the early decades of the 20th century, liberalism, also called "modernism," infiltrated the seminaries of many mainline Protestant denominations in North America, including the Northern Baptist Convention. In time, the fundamentalist–modernist controversy was felt throughout the churches and the mission fields of the world. The controversy centered primarily in the inspiration of the scriptures. One influential liberal was quoted as saying he read his Bible the way he ate fish. He ate the meat and left the bones. This promoted a cafeteria-like approach to biblical doctrine; enjoy what you like and reject what you don't like.

The Northern Baptist Convention (now called the American Baptist Churches) soon had a mixture of liberals and fundamentalists in their churches and on their mission fields. One of their missionaries wrote, "Atonement must go. It remains for us to make our own atonement by living the best life we can. It was not necessary for Jesus to die." The Association of Baptists for World Evangelism, Inc. (ABWE) was born in the Philippines as an authentically biblical alternative to the increasingly liberal theological bias of the denomination from which it came.

Medical doctor Raphael C. Thomas, a Northern Baptist Convention missionary in the Philippines, was motivated by the deep-seated Biblical conviction that all men would be lost forever unless they received Jesus, the Son of God, as their personal Lord and Savior. To Dr. Thomas, medicine was a means to an end. Evangelism and church planting were his goals.

Raphael had been in the Philippines approximately 25 years and was in charge of the mission hospital at Jaro, Iloilo. He also loved to take Filipino pastors-in-training to do evangelism in the province. Eventually this became a point of conflict when some of his fellow workers criticized him for not spending enough time in the hospital. Complaints were made against him to the home board. Finally, a directive came from the general secretary ordering him to cease his evangelism and confine himself to medical work. Raphael felt he could not do this and decided he could no longer continue under that yoke.

Early in 1927 Dr. Thomas returned to the United States for furlough. He appealed to the general secretary for a hearing about the issue but was refused. He then submitted his resignation. In the providence of God, if this had not happened, there might never have been an ABWE!

Dr. Thomas' momentous decision started a chain reaction. He was married to Norma Peabody, whose mother, Lucy (Mrs. Henry W. Peabody), served for 18 years as secretary of the Baptist Women's Foreign Missions Society. When she learned of the unfair treatment the Thomases received, she promptly resigned from her convention duties. Mrs. Marguerite Doane, a lifelong friend of the Thomases and Peabodys, was also greatly disturbed by what had happened. She and her sister had inherited a fortune from their inventor and hymn-writer father, William Howard Doane, and were supporting a number of Baptist missionaries including Raphael and Norma Thomas in the Philippines. The sisters also were now inclined to shift their allegiance, and thus were poised to help a new fledgling mission organization.

Three coworkers, Ellen Martien, Helen Hinkley, and Bessie Traber, confided to Raphael and Norma that if the Thomases resigned or left the field, they would also leave. Another woman, Alice Drake, was a Bible school graduate who had spent enough time at Iloilo to form a lasting friendship with this group of Baptist missionaries. She indicated her oneness with them and said, "If a real break comes, and you need my help in starting a new work, let me know. I'll come back and help you."

On a sunny August day in 1927 Mrs. Doane invited a dozen concerned friends, including the Peabodys, the Thomases, and Dr. Curtis Lawes, editor of the well-known *Watchman Examiner,* to her summer home in Watch Hill, Rhode Island. After discussing whether or not to abandon the Philippine work to theological liberals, they knelt to pray. Out of this prayer meeting came the united conviction to start a new Baptist work in the Philippines. Mrs. Peabody assumed the chair of the new sponsoring committee. A Boston lawyer, Frederick Crawford, agreed to become the secretary and to draw up the papers of incorporation. Hilda Olson served as the first treasurer. Curtis Lawes was in full support of the new entity and promised to publicize it fully in his periodical. Mrs. Doane agreed to serve as chairman of the Finance Committee, a position she held until her death in 1954. A new missionary society had been born. The name chosen was the *Association of Baptists for the Evangelism of the Orient, Inc. (ABEO).*

The mission's new name was carefully selected. It was to be an *association*, rather than a convention, to indicate a voluntary banding together of like-minded missionaries. The missionaries were to be *Baptists*, their primary task was to be *evangelism*, and their field of endeavor would be enlarged to cover the *Orient*.

Two

The First Decade

The fledgling mission decided to begin its work in Iloilo and Manila, quitting the comity agreement by which different missions agree to work in assigned areas. The newly formed ABEO missionaries did not want to abandon the Iloilo field to the liberal Baptists. Besides, the nationals loved Raphael and Norma and pled with them to return. The die was cast. Ellen Martien resigned from the Baptist Convention to join the new group. Bessie Traber cabled Alice Drake (who was then in Egypt). True to her word, Alice returned to Iloilo. This gave ABEO five missionaries the first year: Raphael and Norma Thomas, Ellen Martien, Bessie Traber, and Alice Drake. Helen Hinkley joined the team after her furlough.

The work began to take shape almost immediately when Mrs. Doane authorized first the rental, and later the purchase, of a key piece of property in Iloilo city for a Bible Institute. The building was named Doane Hall in memory of her father. A number of students enrolled. The work was off to a flying start.

When the Thomases returned to the Philippines in 1928, Raphael was determined to start a work in Manila. With funds secured by Mrs. Peabody, he rented property adjacent to the University of the Philippines campus. Later that year he organized the First Baptist Church of Manila with 32 members, many of whom were Christian college students he had known from the Visayas.

Mrs. Doane and her sister felt they should also do something in

Manila in memory of their father. They purchased property only a block or two from the First Baptist Church. There they established the Doane Dormitory for girls who would attend the Manila Evangelistic Institute. Ellen Martien took charge of this dormitory. Others followed her in this position, including Bernice Hahn, Bethel France, and Evelyn Congleton.

In October 1928 the mission was officially incorporated in America when 12 board members signed the incorporation document. In this important procedure, care was taken to avoid the possibility of a ruling hierarchy. The board members could serve one year and be reelected or changed. Additional board members could be added as the mission grew. An Executive Committee of seven was to meet monthly to handle current business.

In the fall of 1929 the first official mission publication was released under the title *Association of Baptists for Evangelism in the Orient, Inc.* The sub-caption read, "*Based on New Testament Method and Message*." In 1932 the publication simply became *The Message*. In that same year the mission opened its first office on the 7th floor of the Schaff building located at 15th and Race streets in Philadelphia. In 1971, by the time ABWE moved to Cherry Hill, New Jersey, the mission occupied almost the entire 13th floor.

Meanwhile, the work in the Philippines continued to grow. New missionaries including Dr. Paul Culley and Margaret Scheirich (who later became Mrs. Culley), Bernice Hahn, and Edith Webster joined the team. Dr. Russell Jones resigned his pulpit in Baltimore to become pastor of the First Baptist Church of Manila. This move freed Raphael for other duties. New missionaries added to the mission in those early years included Captain Ellis and Ruth Skolfield, Bethel France, Alexander Sutherland, Stella Mower, Ruth Woodworth, Esther Yerger, Bernard Bancroft, Edward and Marian Bomm, and Eleanore Bailey (who later became Mrs. Bancroft).

Under the comity agreement, the Presbyterians had been allotted more territory than they were able to handle. Their leader, a good friend of Raphael Thomas, was aware of the new mission agency and offered the Palawan territory to ABEO to evangelize. The proposal was put in writing and sent to the home board. At a November 1930 meeting, the board voted unanimously to accept the offer.

The province of Palawan consisted of nearly 100 islands at the extreme end of the archipelago. The most practical way to evangelize such an area would be with a seaworthy boat. Enter Captain Ellis Skolfield. Mrs. Peabody's minutes begin the story: "Heavenly wireless is not slow!" The following day after the November meeting, three members of the committee met Captain and Mrs. Ellis Skolfield in Philadelphia. Ellis was deeply interested in the Philippines through his association in Philadelphia with Bessie Traber and Alice Drake. This couple was accepted, and within months the Skolfields sailed for Manila where he began teaching in the Bible institute and helping in general missionary work.

Some months after the Skolfields arrived in Manila, Raphael received a letter from a Baptist missionary in Japan. He wanted to know if ABEO could use a boat in their ministry. He mentioned that they no longer needed the gospel ship called the *Fukuin Maru*. Was this an answer to prayer? Raphael viewed the offer as "nothing ventured, nothing gained" and decided to look into it. First there had been the gift of the islands to evangelize, then the coming of a fully qualified sea captain, and now the availability of a boat!

With board approval, Ellis went to Japan to inspect the boat being offered for $14,000. It was 120 feet long, 24 feet wide, built of wood with copper sheeting covering the hull. It had an auxiliary oil-burning engine generating a speed of nine knots. There was also a smaller auxiliary engine for generating electricity. The ship had two kitchen stoves, three two-berth cabins for passengers, four one-berth cabins, and a six-berth cabin for the crew. It had two 400-gallon fuel tanks and other equipment, including a six-foot-square medical dispensary.

Captain Skolfield was authorized to make the purchase. The deal was closed at $10,000—the exact amount Mrs. Peabody had received from her friend Mary Colgate. The board approved an additional $5,000 to renovate the ship before sailing it to Manila. That first voyage was a squeaker. Ellis and his crew nearly lost the ship in a storm as they neared Manila, but God spared them.

After surveying the province of Palawan, Captain Skolfield chose the little island of Cuyo as headquarters for the ship's ministry. Mrs. Doane agreed to buy land and build a house there. Rev. Harold Commons, ABEO's new president, spent the month of February 1936 on board the ship observing firsthand what was being accomplished. He was greatly impressed.

But problems developed. Funding for the project diminished because of the Great Depression years. When rich deposits of manganese ore were discovered in Palawan, Captain Skolfield devised a plan to take advantage of the situation as a way to fund his ministry. He was bitten, however, by the get-rich-quick bug and was soon into a business venture of sizable proportions. When the board learned that the ship was now being called the "Manganese Ship" instead of the "Gospel Ship" they called Captain Skolfield home. His repentance was genuine but, later when the board could no longer fund the ministry due to the impending world war, Ellis resigned and rejoined the navy as port captain of the port of Manila.

The "Gospel Ship" did yeoman service in the Philippines for nearly ten years before the ministry was abandoned and the ship donated to the U.S. Navy. The purpose for which God had given the ship to ABEO had been largely fulfilled. A gospel witness had been established in every municipality of the province. During the six years of the ship's service in Palawan, over 1,000 believers were baptized and 14 churches organized with faithful Filipino pastors in charge. The Palawan Association of Fundamental Baptist

Churches had been formed. Several missionaries were resident in the province when the war intervened.

During the first decade of ABEO's existence, Bible institutes were started at both Iloilo and Manila. Infant churches were established throughout the Visayas and on the islands of Panay, Guimaras, and Negros. On the island of Luzon the work spread from Manila to other towns and barrios in the province of Rizal. Missionary personnel and the home board felt keenly that they had the responsibility before God to do everything possible to reach people for Christ.

Mrs. Doane purchased land and built a vacation rest home at Baguio in northern Luzon. This led to the establishment of work among the famous headhunters of the mountain province, the Igorots and Bontocs.

In 1937 Henry and Gladys DeVries and Rhoda Little, who had been independent missionaries, brought their work on the island of Mindanao into the new mission. Starting with the province of Bukidnon, in time the mission moved into the provinces of Cagayan and Davao, as well. Rhoda Little and Gladys DeVries, trained nurses, began a medical clinic at Malaybalay which, after WW II, became the Bethel Baptist Hospital, under the direction of Dr. Lincoln Nelson. With God's blessing, ABEO made a substantial contribution to the evangelization of the Philippines in those early years.

On the home front, ABEO's first decade brought new direction and policy changes that continue until today. The mission suffered criticism from the Northern Baptist Convention, which saw the new agency as a disgruntled group supported by a few wealthy women and destined for failure. But God had other plans. While the Great Depression played havoc with many missions, ABEO became the recipient of a $100,000 gift from the will of Miss Mary Colgate. She left a permanent fund from which the interest could be used for the general work of the mission. The Depression, however, made ABEO realize the need for broadening their base of support with a healthy balance between individual and church donors.

Shaping the mission's financial policy became a priority. First, the board decided ABEO would be a *faith* Baptist mission. They felt the term *faith* should not be monopolized by inter- or nondenominational mission agencies. Secondly, the principle of operating debt free became the cornerstone of ABEO's financial policy. Lastly, the board rejected the system of pooling missionary support funds in preference to the concept of individual missionary support. This would be a way to honor the wishes of individual donors. Tax receipts would be issued for support, outfit and passage, and work funds, but not for personal gifts.

During this first decade, ABEO's doctrinal position regarding the Second Coming of Christ was finalized. Confusion and controversy arose in the Philippines between some of the older missionaries who held the postmillennial view and the newer ones who were premillennialists. This led the board to appoint a study committee that came up with a premillennial statement emphasizing the belief of the imminent return of Christ. The board voted unanimously that ABEO would be a premillennial, Baptist, fundamental, faith mission. While a few missionaries resigned or took other ministry opportunities, calm was restored to troubled waters.

Finally, the decade brought change into the governing structure of ABEO. Mrs. Lucy Peabody served as president for seven years, after which she resigned in favor of Rev. Harold T. Commons. In a resignation letter she said, "My major reasons for resigning are the propriety and wisdom of electing a man to fill this important office since it deals with churches and pastors, as well as with questions which properly belong to masculine leadership in the church."

Harold Commons resigned the pulpit of the First Baptist Church of Johnson City, New York, to assume the presidency of

ABEO in 1935. At that time there were 18 missionaries serving in one country: the Philippines. It became obvious to him that the long-range financial stability of the mission lay not with individuals but with churches. He took to the road representing the mission work through public ministry, films, slides, and literature, with a view to broadening the base of support. In taking this new direction Rev. Commons expressed his heartfelt appreciation for Mrs. Doane, Mrs. Peabody, and Miss Colgate for their financial input into the mission, which provided economic financial stability during its first decade of its existence.

Three

Expansion Efforts in Asia

PAPUA NEW GUINEA

Feeling that the mission should broaden its horizons beyond the Philippines, the board appointed an Expansion Committee to investigate other possibilities in Asia. Consideration was given to using the "Gospel Ship" on the Mekong River in French Indochina (now Cambodia, Laos, and Vietnam). In consultations with the Christian and Missionary Alliance, which knew the area well, they discouraged the idea, and the matter was dropped. The Expansion Committee then approved a survey trip into other areas.

In 1939 and 1940 Captain Ellis Skolfield and Dr. Paul Culley surveyed the Celebes and Moluccas, and along the north coast of New Guinea as far as Hollandia. After Captain Skolfield's resignation from the mission to join the Navy, Dr. Culley made a second trip to Dutch New Guinea. He traveled into the interior as far as the Wissel Lakes and contacted the primitive Kopauko tribe.

The mission decided to begin working in New Guinea, but two things delayed the plans. Dr. Culley, the most likely missionary to open the field, wanted to drop Baptist from the mission's name. When the Board disagreed, the Culleys resigned after 12 fruitful years of service. The second delay was that World War II engulfed the East Indian Archipelago. Expansion plans for New Guinea had to be put on hold.

After the war, interest to penetrate the interior of New Guinea rekindled. Fourteen missionaries applied and were accepted in 1945 with this field in mind. They included Robert and Frances

Burns, William and Ethel Goldie, Stanley and Martha Jean Holman, Robert and Elaine Banning, Dr. Link and Lenore Nelson, Gerald Rose, and Campbell and Lois Murdoch. Mrs. Doane promised to purchase and equip a plane and a jeep for the project.

The Henry DeVries family, who spoke Dutch fluently and who already had 25 years of missionary experience, made themselves available to help open the field. The Dutch government, however, refused to allow the mission to enter New Guinea because of a movement among nationals for self-government. After three years, dreams for an airplane ministry in Dutch New Guinea were laid to rest. The Robert Burnses applied for a transfer to South America. The Goldies, Bannings, Holmans, and Nelsons were temporarily assigned to the Philippines until New Guinea opened.

In 1967 interest in New Guinea revived when independent Baptist missionaries, Mr. and Mrs. Howell Williams, made an urgent appeal for help. They were working in the mid-island capital of Goroka, and offered to turn over their work to ABWE. The need was made known to the churches and missionary family. David and Joan Gardner, on furlough from the Philippines and uncertain about a future ministry, responded with interest. After a meeting with the ABWE Executive Committee, permission was given for Dave Gardner to make a trip to Goroka to meet the Williamses and see the situation firsthand.

His report was favorable, and on September 11, 1967, the board unanimously voted "to enter New Guinea as a mission field, and to assign David and Joan Gardner as the first ABWE missionaries to Papua New Guinea."

UPDATE 2000 Many ABWE missionaries have served effectively in Papua New Guinea, focusing on church-planting and theological education in the Highlands provinces of Simbu, Eastern Highlands, Western Highlands, and Madang. Goroka Baptist Bible College trains pastors and lay leaders for the churches.

At least 50 churches have been planted by ABWE missionaries and nationals. Aviation ministries make it possible to plant churches in remote areas. Specialized evangelism is conducted through campus ministries, literacy training, and youth work.

CEYLON

In 1937 ABEO's Committee on Expansion came in contact with Rev. and Mrs. James Ker, independent Baptists working in Colombo. Because the Ceylon and India General Mission had closed their work in Ceylon, the Kers applied to the ABWE and were appointed. They were to continue their ministry at the Ceylon Bible Training Center in Colombo. However, less than a year later, Mrs. Ker's health failed, causing them to return home. She never regained sufficient health to return to the field. After working for a short time with Dr. Commons in the mission office, Jim felt led to take a pastorate.

A young couple, Rev. and Mrs. Robert Arthur, had heard Jim Ker speak and were impressed with the great needs in Ceylon. They volunteered and were appointed in October 1941. War erupted in Asia causing a four-year delay in their departure. The harrowing trip to Ceylon, the post-war conditions, and the fact that six years had elapsed since the Kers' departure and that the Arthurs would have to start from scratch, caused great frustration. The Arthurs resigned, and Ceylon faded away as a field of ABWE.

Four

Moving Into South America—and a New Name

PERU

During 1938 and 1939 William and Elva Scherer, independent Baptist missionaries on furlough from the Amazon Valley in Peru, stayed at the Houses of Fellowship in Ventnor, New Jersey. They, like hundreds of other missionaries, benefited from Mrs. Doane's generosity of free housing. After viewing their slides and hearing of their dissatisfaction working as independent missionaries, Mrs. Doane recommended them to the ABEO's Committee on Expansion. After a May 1939 interview, their appointment looked certain. Action was deferred one month, however, to legally change the name of the organization.

The June 1939 official minutes recorded two actions: Voted #610 to "change the name of this corporation from the *Association of Baptists for Evangelism in the Orient* to the *Association of Baptists for World Evangelism*," and Voted #611 "that Rev. and Mrs. William Scherer be accepted as missionaries of this Association."

For seven years before joining ABWE, the Scherers had lived in the village of Pevas, Peru, in the Upper Amazon. They chose a 300-mile stretch of river flowing from the town of Iquitos to the Brazilian border. Instead of settling in Iquitos, they carved out a mission station at Pevas near the area of the Yahua and Witoto Indian tribes. Ernie Olsen, who had helped the Scherers build the station, also joined ABWE, as did Harry and Wilma Stahlman who had earlier worked in Iquitos.

These missionaries established a Bible institute in Iquitos. Since their work area extended from Iquitos to Leticia, Colombia, on the border of Brazil, they decided to divide the area into the Upper and Central Amazon field councils.

In 1957 ABWE saw the need to have representation in Lima, the capital city of Peru, to facilitate the entrance of new missionaries into the country. The Scherers along with the Olsens established the Coastal Peru field council, which today includes the cities of Lima and Arequipa.

UPDATE 2000 From the wilds of the jungle to the heights of the mountains, to the throngs of the city streets, Peru presents a fertile mission field ripe for harvest. ABWE's Peruvian work began in the Amazon basin. Launch evangelism has extended the ministry up and down the Amazon River and its tributaries. The city of Iquitos is home to the Iquitos Baptist Bible Institute, which trains local people for church leadership. Autonomous Baptist churches now form the basis for missionary outreach. ABWE works in the capital city of Lima and in Arequipa, the second largest city. Building relationships through personal contacts and Bible studies, the missionaries are advancing the gospel among business and professional people. Another opportunity for witness is in an outreach to the interior of the Andes Mountains. Much work in Peru is now done in partnership with local churches and pastors.

BRAZIL

ABWE's entrance into Brazil in 1942 was not the result of a plan but of circumstances. A small group of independent Baptist missionaries called the Gospel Furtherance Band of Brazil experienced the same unhappiness working with a nondenominational mission board as had the Scherers in the Upper Amazon. The group of four couples, three of whom belonged to the same family, was led by Carleton Matthews and his wife, Mary Adelaide. During the 1930's Mrs. Matthews' brother, Robert Standley, and his wife joined them as did a younger brother, Gerald, and his wife. A fourth couple, the Davises, also joined the group.

In 1940 Rev. Ralph Standley, pastor of the Baptist church in Appleton, New York, and father of the three Standleys in Brazil, visited the ABWE office in Philadelphia. He proposed to Dr. Commons that the Gospel Furtherance Band merge with ABWE so the larger organization could sponsor and lend strength to their work. This proposal presented a problem ABWE couldn't accept. As proposed, the relationship would be only an affiliation. The idea was turned down.

A year later, Carleton Matthews, who was on furlough, visited Harold Commons. Dr. Commons explained that ABWE's Principles and Practices requires all missionaries to be on the same level, with each individual meeting ABWE requirements and being directly responsible to the board. Mr. Matthews took this information back to Brazil. Eventually, the Gospel Furtherance Band was dissolved.

The area where these missionaries had been working was in the semi-barren state of Rio Grande do Norte, on the hump of northeast Brazil. This became the first ABWE field in Brazil. The Robert Standleys were the first missionaries appointed at the October 1942 board meeting.

The opening into Brazil came as a fresh breeze to ABWE. The Philippines was closed due to the war, and some of the missionaries had been interned by the Japanese. Doors were closed to New Guinea and Ceylon. The Robert Burnses and Donald Davises couldn't go to Peru because the Peruvian government wouldn't grant visas to new missionaries. But then Brazil opened. Work there was already established and had seasoned personnel. The Carleton Matthewses were resident in Saõ Jose du Mibibu, where he had planted and was pastoring a church. The Standleys returned to their former station at Mossoro, in the interior. New ABWE missionaries joined to help develop the work. They included Misses Virginia LeSuer and Dorothy Palmer, followed by Donald and Helen Hare, who had been unable to enter the Philippines due to the war.

Carl and Mary Adelaide Matthews officially joined ABWE in the spring of 1944. Because of his connections as chaplain to the United States Air Force base outside Natal, he was able to acquire an old army barracks and recreation facility on the shore of Lake Bom Fim. This facility has served as a campground and conference center for missionaries. As the work grew, property was secured in the capital city of Natal, where the missionaries established Berean Baptist Bible College. Throughout the years, many national pastors and evangelists received their training there.

In 1946, Don and Helen Hare arrived in Natal. Three months later their young son, Bobby, died of an unknown fever. When their daughter also became ill, the Hares moved south to the megalopolis of Saõ Paulo. God spared her life, and today she and two of her sisters are ABWE missionaries. Don Hare started the Baptist Bible Seminary and Institute (now known as the Regular Baptist Seminary) in Saõ Paulo. Art and Joyce Cavey and Mel and Dorothy Cuthbert joined the Hares to engage in church planting and national leadership education. Scores of churches have been planted and are pastored by well-trained Brazilians.

As personnel increased, missionary work expanded into the state of Pernambuco, beginning with the capital city of Recife and extending to interior towns. The transfer of Kenneth and Jean Mitchell to Bahia resulted in the formation of the Coastal Brazil field council.

UPDATE 2000 ABWE works in seven areas of this vast country. The Regular Baptist Press in Saõ Paulo produces Portuguese-language materials that benefit not only Brazilians, but also

Portuguese-speaking people throughout the world. What began as a support ministry for church growth in Brazil is now an outreach in its own right, providing Christian literature in countries such as Angola, the Azores, and Portugal.

Missionaries and local believers in Brazil are involved in church planting, theological education, literature production and distribution, medical evangelism, aviation, camps, Christian counseling, ministry to the hearing-impaired, and MK education.

[Don and Helen Hare wrote an illustrated children's story based on their evangelistic outreach in Saõ Paulo. Order *Kidnapped* from ABWE Publishing.]

COLOMBIA

ABWE had been unsuccessful in getting visas for the Davises and the Burnses to join the Scherers in the Upper Amazon. They could, however, get visas for Colombia, where they could reach the Amazon River at Leticia. Once again, Mrs. Doane donated funds for the Scherers to buy a house in Leticia in readiness for the Davises' arrival. The Burnses followed after completing language study in Medellin.

About this time, the James Carders came to ABWE to work in the highlands of Colombia. The Carders had previously worked with the Orinoco River Mission in Venezuela until Jim developed a lung condition due to the severe tropical climate. They then went as independent missionaries to the Canary Islands, where they served faithfully for seven more years until the war forced them out. The Carders then joined ABWE with a special interest in Colombia. For health reasons they decided to work in a high, dry climate.

The Carders stayed with ABWE for three years, working in both Colombia and Venezuela, but felt no leading to settle in either place. Later, the door opened for them to return to the

Canary Islands. Since ABWE felt that it would be spreading itself too thin for the mission to enter the Canary Islands, the Carders submitted their resignation.

UPDATE 2000 ABWE's first church in Colombia was established in 1942 in the city of Leticia, situated on the southern tip of Colombia along the Amazon River. For the next 25 years, a launch ministry extended the work to several preaching stations along the Colombian shores of the Amazon. In the early 1970's aviation evangelism extended the outreach to a 300-mile radius north of Leticia.

In 1977 the Colombian government closed the jungle mission stations to expatriate missionaries. ABWE had already begun work in Bogotá, Colombia's capital, so that city became the center of operation. Churches planted in the 1970's now have their own buildings and national pastors, and several branch churches are in formation. Camp, VBS, personal contacts, and Bible studies are some of the methods used. Training of national leaders takes place through the Bible institute, a four-year night school started in 1980, which is supplemented by the TEE program of learning. The Bogotá Christian Academy provides education for missionary children grades one through twelve.

The violent activity of powerful drug cartels has greatly limited their outreach, yet the ABWE missionaries say, "We are overwhelmed by what God is doing in Colombia."

THE BIRTH OF ABWE'S AVIATION MINISTRY

Robert Standley used a plane in his work in northeast Brazil, but the plane had to be sold to pay his debts. On arrival home for furlough, Bob submitted his resignation.

An aviation ministry became all the more important, however, as the fields in South America developed. The Upper Amazon work extended several hundred miles down the Amazon River. Leticia, Colombia, was an open port and enjoyed friendlier relations with Brazil than with Peru. With ABWE's approval, the state of Amazonas in Colombia was combined with a stretch of 800 miles along the Amazon in Brazil to comprise the Amazonas field council. John and Fran Schlener and Paul and Jessie Schlener settled at the Port of Two Brothers in Brazil to work among the Ticuna Indians. Lindsey and Jean Harrell, Edward and Dorothy Blakslee, and others developed mission stations in Brazil at remote points on the river.

Pilot Henry (Hank) Scheltema and his wife, Ruth, were appointed to ABWE in October 1958. In early 1961, after raising adequate funds, he purchased a four-place, single engine, Aeronica pontoon plane and flew it to the Amazon. He based it in Benjamin Constant in Brazil, just across the river from Leticia, Colombia. Brazil was the only one of the three countries that would grant permission for civilian aviation. When another pilot and plane became necessary, the Terry Bowers family joined the Scheltemas. In the 1960's and 1970's two more pilots and planes were added, and the aviation ministry was extended up the Putumayo River into Colombia. Donald and Janice Fanning and Butch and Bonnie Jarvis spearheaded this work, reaching places where the gospel had never been heard. When the Colombian government's policy changed in 1977, aviation work stopped.

UPDATE 2000 Hank Scheltema was appointed ABWE International Administrator of Aviation in 1981. Hank's daughter Kim and her pilot husband, Al Yoder, joined with the Scheltemas in the aviation work. During Hank's years of experience he developed ABWE's approach to missionary aviation. Pilots are also to be church planters or church-planting assistants in addition to their aviation work. They are responsible for raising their own support and all expenses incurred in their ministry, depending on God's supply of their needs. ABWE's airbase is located in Concord, Georgia, where new aviation appointees are screened and prepared for ministry.

[Be sure to read:

- *Jungle Myths: The Story of ABWE's Medical Work Along The Amazon*, by Keith Kaynor
- *The Port of Two Brothers*, by Paul Schlener

Both books are available through ABWE Publishing.]

Five

War in the Philippines

The Pacific war reached the Philippines in December 1942. The bombing of Manila started December 10. When Manila fell to the Japanese, all Western expatriates, including the missionaries, were rounded up, registered, questioned, and temporarily released to their homes. Only the leaders of the various organizations, including ABWE's Edward Bomm, were isolated and interned. These leaders were summoned before the Japanese military commander and required to sign a pledge of cooperation with the Japanese that promised peace and prosperity to all. Some of the missionary leaders signed, but Ed Bomm refused. As a result, the Japanese separated Ed from his wife, Marian, and imprisoned him in Los Baños for over three years.

Marian Bomm was also suspected of subversive activity in aiding the Filipino Underground Resistance Movement. She was arrested and confined for 72 days in the infamous Fort Santiago dungeon, and later taken to Santo Tomas.

As the war progressed, all expatriates were either interned or imprisoned in guarded camps. Three of the four biggest camps, Santo Tomas, Bilibid Prison, and the infamous Spanish dungeon of Fort Santiago were in Manila. Los Baños was located a few miles to the southeast of Manila. ABWE's history of this period records many stories of the missionaries' pain and praise, of their sufferings and sorrows, and, in the end, of their release.

An amazing part of this story centers on the goodness and thoughtfulness of former ABWE missionary Captain Ellis Skolfield. He was the American naval officer left behind to blow up the U.S. naval base at Cavite on Manila Bay just prior to the Japanese takeover. Before touching off the final charge of explosives, Ellis loaded a two-ton military truck with canned goods and food supplies and drove to the Bible institute, where Ruth Woodworth was in charge. With a cheery grin, he said to Ruth, "Here, this stuff may save your lives before this thing is over. Hide all you can and distribute the rest to your fellow missionaries with my compliments." His prediction came true.

ABWE missionaries Ruth Woodworth, Evelyn Congleton, and Mona Kemery were in Manila when the war started, and were later interned there. Esther Yerger and Edna Hotchkiss fled to Baguio. Helen Hinkley and Elsie Parks hid out in the mountains of Panay but eventually turned themselves in for internment. Palawan missionaries, the F. W. (Bernie) Naylor family and Elsie Howell, remained at their posts until the Japanese took over the islands. Elsie fled to the hills, where she married a national and lived safely during the war. Henry DeVries' oldest son, David, a student in Manila, was interned in Los Baños. His parents, sister Gene, and brother Buddy, who lived on the island of Mindanao, were later arrested and united with David in the same camp. Paul and Kay Friederichsen were also interned there.

Robert and Grace Kohler and Louise Lynip were the only ABWE missionaries who successfully eluded the Japanese. They hid in the mountains of Mindanao and managed to escape on an American submarine to Australia, and from there back to the United States.

ABWE missionaries, for the most part, lived without being tortured or harassed. As the war dragged on, however, they suffered from hunger and near nakedness. Early on, the food supplied by Ellis Skolfield met some of their needs. But, they eventually had to exist on the meager rations given to them by their captors. Beriberi and pellagra, diseases often caused by malnutrition, afflicted many in the POW camps. Before liberation, many missionaries killed and ate the cats and rats that entered their compound!

The first and only ABWE missionary to die during the war was Harold Palmer who was interned in Baguio. After ten months in the prison camp he suffered an attack of appendicitis. Even though the operation was performed by a capable American surgeon, he died ten days after surgery. Harold's inability to fight off infection may have been related to his weakened condition from an unbalanced diet.

In February 1945 General Douglas MacArthur's troops liberated the Philippines. ABWE missionaries burst forth with emotional praise. Elsie Parks wrote on February 6, "Not only has our army come and freed us; they've also brought food. You should see it—truck after truck loaded with good things to eat. It seems unbelievable. And, they brought us mail!" Kay Friederichsen wrote on February 7, 1945, "Yes, it's really over! The sky is black with smoke and fire; guns are booming, shrapnel falling, but we are free!"

When the Los Baños camp was liberated, Ruth Woodworth wrote, "The parachute troops descended from the sky. The Japanese started running. Bullets were flying all around (we hid under the bed). Suddenly a big amphibious tank appeared right beside our barracks with the shout to prepare our stuff and be ready to leave in five minutes!"

Fifteen-year-old Buddy DeVries described the liberation to an uncle in Grand Rapids, Michigan. "Boy, oh boy! It sure is nice to be free. The shooting started. What a racket! Mom, Gene, Dad and I got in the air raid shelter we had made in our cook shack. After the American soldiers entered our camp, one soldier told us to pack as quickly as possible. We were sent to the ball field where the Am-tracks were waiting. On the tank a soldier opened a box of field rations. Nothing had ever tasted so good to me in all my life. I am 15 years old. In October last year I weighed 110 pounds.

Now I weigh only 78 pounds."

After liberation, Ed Bomm was reunited with his wife, Marian. He wrote, "I hardly recognized her when she came in, but she is alive. We have much to thank God for." The Bomms didn't want to return to the United States until they had inspected ABWE property. Mr. Bomm's decision reflected his spirit of dedication to ABWE and world evangelism. Missionary Samuel Fisk paid this fitting tribute to Ed Bomm: "The heads of the missionary societies in Manila were called before the Japanese military commanders and asked to sign a prepared statement. To sign would involve first, reducing the Christian faith to the level of all religions generally; secondly, it would mean submitting the churches under our care in the Philippines to a position of political servitude.

"It took courage and faith when Ed Bomm refused to sign because he didn't know what his refusal would entail. For him, as it turned out, it meant more than three years of separation from his wife. It meant three years of confinement to a limited, congested area where barbed wire and armed sentries formed part of the monotonous scenery, and where food and ordinary conveniences were insufficient.

"Ed rose in stature and favor in the eyes of the interned American business people and before the entire Filipino community. The Religious Activities Committee of Santo Tomas Camp was reorganized and Ed was placed at the head of all religious activities which involved planning services for 4000 internees. Furthermore, his courageous stand, in which he represented all of the missionaries, has had a profound effect on national pastors and churches. The entire work of the ABWE stands in a commendable position, and will undoubtedly enjoy larger opportunities in the post-war period."

[Read the remarkable stories of the Philippine war years in the books *Beyond Prison Walls*, by Marian Bomm, and *No Greater Joy*, by Ruth Woodworth. Both books are available through ABWE Publishing.]

Six

Rebuilding in the Philippines

All the ABWE missionaries, except the Bomms, returned to North America to recuperate as soon as transportation was available. Ed Bomm felt he ought to remain and look after the mission's interests during the critical postwar period. All the ABWE properties had been damaged or destroyed. Property deeds and official records were gone. It was necessary to file claims for prewar real estate and to reestablish ownership with the Bureau of Lands. He also wanted to reestablish contact with the Filipino leaders and pastors and to encourage them in every way possible. The Bible institute was gone. The First Baptist Church was gone. Doane dormitory was gone. Yet in these discouraging circumstances the Lord reassured the mission of His sovereign control.

In December 1941 the Philippine government had expropriated a piece of land and a building owned by ABWE. They arbitrarily took the property and gave the mission 75,000 pesos in payment. The building, named the Friendly Center, had been an effective tool for reaching Filipinos for Christ. The war had already started, and the law and order situation grew worse by the day. Something had to be done with the 75,000 pesos, so Ed Bomm and field council treasurer Bob Smallwood deposited the cash in bank lock box #184 and walked out with the key.

The Japanese soon occupied Manila and took firm control of everything, including the banks. During his internment, Ed Bomm often thought about that money. He reasoned that what thieves didn't steal, the Japanese certainly would. He prayed for the safety of the money, and committed the matter to the Lord.

About a year later, the Japanese announced that internees could have access to their safe deposit boxes if they had the proper credentials and a key. Afraid to go himself, Ed sent a Filipino friend to check out this news. His messenger returned with a discouraging report: people who stood in line to get their possessions, returned from the vault empty-handed. Rumor had it that the deposit boxes had been emptied.

On February 1, 1945, after the U.S. Army liberated the Philippines, one of the first things that came to Ed's mind was deposit box #184. In his own words, "It was November 1945 before authorization was received for me to access the vault. Then with a bond official and a Filipino helper carrying a chisel and hammer, I went to box #184. My helper severed the hinges and I removed the inner box. I took inventory and counted the pesos. The contents of the box were exactly as they had been in December 1941!" This money provided the missionaries with a new start.

American G.I.'s were everywhere in the city. In their free time they had nowhere to go and nothing to do but get into trouble. Having met some excellent American chaplains and a good number of Christians among the servicemen, Ed and Marian started a Christian Service Center for U.S. military personnel. The work grew so quickly they had to find larger accommodations.

During the week the Bomms conducted Bible studies. The G.I. Gospel Hour on Saturday nights proved to be a great evangelistic tool. One serviceman wrote, "I have been going to the gospel rally every Saturday evening and between 400 and 500 G.I.'s, WAC's, sailors, nurses and Red Cross workers attend." The godly lives of Ed and Marian Bomm impressed many people.

In November 1945 a temporary prefab building was erected on the site of ABWE's former Bible institute and First Baptist Church. This larger facility became the new location for the G.I.

Gospel Hour. By this time, between 500 to 600 attended the meetings. The G.I.'s who helped finance and build the new facility built an apartment on the rear of the building for the Bomms. Ed and Marian lived there until furlough in June 1946, by which time Sam Fisk, Edwin and Helen Spahr, Sadie Busse, and the Bernard Bancroft family had all returned to Manila. Robert and Grace Kohler, Louise Lynip, and Jean Wagner had returned to Malaybalay, Mindanao. Eventually, most of the prewar missionaries returned and new appointees joined the work.

A major problem developed shortly after the Bomm's G.I. ministry moved onto ABWE property. Up until then, the G.I. work was a nondenominational basis. Before long, however, some of the servicemen began dreaming of establishing an Asian Moody Bible Institute type of school in the Philippines to be sponsored by the Far Eastern Gospel Crusade. Since ABWE already had a building in Manila, the servicemen wanted Ed Bomm to head up the school.

ABWE administration saw problems with this arrangement. Baptist and separatist convictions would be unwelcome in a nondenominational school. The board regretfully declined to cooperate. The G.I.'s then bought land in a suburb of Manila and built their own school. ABWE maintained friendly relations with the school, but no organic connection.

Eventually, funds were received from the Philippine government under the War Damage Claims Program. These funds made it possible to tear down the prefab tabernacle and rebuild the First Baptist Church and seminary building. The newly built school was named the Baptist Bible Seminary and Institute. William Hopewell, Jr., became the first director. In 1959–60 the seminary moved to its own premises in the Taytay suburb of Manila.

Another problem arose when Edwin Spahr became pastor of the First Baptist Church in Manila. Edwin began to work closely with Youth for Christ. Robert Cook, the president of Youth for Christ

International at that time, had been Mrs. Spahr's pastor in Philadelphia. The cooperation with other evangelicals of "like precious faith" seemed to be working fine until ABWE missionaries and national believers in Iloilo faced a serious problem of compromise. The situation in Iloilo was different from Manila in that Iloilo was the area originally given to the Baptists under the comity agreement. When Youth for Christ went to Iloilo they sought cooperation from both the ABWE and Convention Baptist churches. Since ABEO had come out of the Convention, individuals felt uneasy cooperating with Youth for Christ. The fact that the Manila missionaries were cooperating escalated their concerns. Nationals accused the mission of having a double standard.

At the April 1948 annual board meeting in Philadelphia, action was taken unanimously reaffirming the mission's historic position of separation, not only from liberals, but from those who closely cooperate with liberals in an inclusive policy. Unfortunately, the Spahrs and Sadie Busse resigned over the decision. The Lord, however, kept the mission from what might have been a blowup of sizable proportions. While much criticism was leveled at the mission, care was taken to point out that the basic motivation was positive, not negative.

As individuals, and as a mission, we seek and enjoy personal fellowship with all members of the body of Christ. The bonds of Christian love are real and precious, for they are eternal. We have been happy to find areas of cooperation with others of like precious faith. One such area has been the education of missionary children. Faith Academy in Manila is a good example of a cooperative project. Missionaries also offer hospitality in their homes and guest facilities, and extend a helping hand wherever they can, as long as that does not involve compromise of doctrines they hold dear.

UPDATE 2000 ABWE was born in Iloilo, on the island of Panay. Since this birth, five regional sub-councils have been created under one All-Philippine Field Council. These councils serve mainly on the islands of Luzon, Palawan, Panay, Leyte, Mindanao, Negros, and Cebu. Only 700 of the Philippines' 7,100 islands are inhabited—only 693 islands left to evangelize!

ABWE missionaries' methods have included tent and open-air evangelism, student centers, and children's ministries to draw people to Christ. Doane Baptist Bible College in Iloilo and the Baptist Bible Seminary and Institute outside Manila have become indigenous, and Filipino leadership has initiated several other Bible colleges throughout the country.

Medicine has also been a tool of evangelism. Medical services began on the island of Mindanao at Bethel Baptist Clinic, where major surgery can be performed. The islands of Leyte, Palawan, and Panay also have medical evangelistic facilities.

The Association of Fundamental Baptist Churches of the Philippines *(AFBCP)* now has nearly 2000 member churches and a foreign mission agency called *PABWE* (Philippine Association of Baptists for World Evangelism). These indigenous churches have demonstrated an ability to plant churches in their home culture, but needs to translate that capability to evangelize, disciple, and start churches in cross-cultural contexts.

For seven decades ABWE has done church planting in the Philippines. Now the driving force will be for missionaries to encourage and equip *Asians to Reach Asia* in cross-cultural ministries, starting with local ethnic groups such as Chinese and Muslims, and extending to nations throughout Southeast Asia and beyond. The Philippines, perhaps more than other Asian nations, represents a tremendous pool of potential Christian workers.

[For further information about the Philippines, be sure to read:

- *With Scalpel and the Sword*, by Dr. Link Nelson
- *Me? A Missionary?* and *A Poetic Interlude*, by Millie Crouch

These books are available through ABWE Publishing.]

Seven

Postwar Expansion in Asia

During the war years, when Asia was closed to missionary activity, the mission directed its energies toward South America. After the war the first priority was to revitalize our Philippine field. Then new developments occurred in rapid succession in other countries of Asia.

SOUTH CHINA

In 1941 ABWE board member Dr. David Otis Fuller, pastor of the Wealthy Street Baptist Church in Grand Rapids, Michigan, and an ABWE board member, mentioned Rev. Victor and Margaret Barnett, who were working independently in the Luichow Peninsula of South China. Feeling the Barnetts would be happier working with ABWE, Dr. Fuller broached the subject with them. They were positive about the idea, but continued their work at Chek Hom until 1943 when the Japanese invaded the area. The Barnetts escaped through free China and returned to the United States. In January of 1945 they met with the ABWE Executive Committee in Philadelphia. After sharing the story of their ministry in China, the Barnetts were unanimously accepted into the missionary family. They returned to Chek Hom early in 1946.

The Barnetts influenced Jaymes and Dorothy Morgan, who had also worked in China for many years, to join ABWE. New recruits for South China also made application to ABWE. In October 1948 Frank and Sophie Jenista, Luella Loewen, and Hedwig

(Hedie) Helsten were appointed to that field. They left in February 1949 to begin Cantonese language study in Chek Hom.

About this time, revolutionary Mao Tse-tung came out of the caves of western China with his followers to seize territories from the Nationalist government of Generalissimo Chiang Kai-shek. Because of the deteriorating political situation in China, the decision was made to have Jay and Dorothy Morgan accompany the new missionaries to Hong Kong, where they could continue language study with peace of mind. The Barnetts stayed on in Chek Hom.

The speedy takeover of China by the communists came as a surprise. By October 1949 the city of Canton had fallen. The safety of the missionaries in Hong Kong became a great concern. After much prayer, the ABWE board voted to let the China missionaries decide for themselves whether to stay where they were or go elsewhere. The Morgans, Jenistas, and Misses Loewen and Helsten transferred to Iloilo in the Philippines, where they were badly needed to teach in the Doane Baptist Bible Institute.

The Barnetts remained at Chek Hom until the communists overran the Luichow Peninsula. They escaped to Hong Kong on a boat full of pigs. They hid among the pigs while soldiers fired at each other across the river. The pigs caught the crossfire and spared the Barnetts' lives.

HONG KONG

Although the missionaries had hoped to remain in China, that was not possible. After their furlough, the Barnetts felt led of the Lord to go to Hong Kong. The communists chose to leave the British Crown Colony alone and use it as their commercial outlet to the outside world. It wasn't long before they set up the largest bank in Hong Kong, the Bank of China.

The Barnetts began to work with the thousands of displaced persons and refugees from the mainland who lived in shantytowns in Kowloon and the New Territories. They worked alone in Hong Kong from 1951 to 1955 when four seasoned missionaries joined them: Bill and Joan Reid, and sisters Ruth and Dortha Warner. Veterans of a term in India when they were denied re-entry visas into India, they made application to ABWE. They were accepted in April 1955 and sent on a temporary assignment to help the Barnetts in Hong Kong. The Hong Kong field began to grow with the arrival of Starling Post, a registered nurse. Jaymes and Dorothy Morgan rejoined the Hong Kong field council after a short-term assignment in Japan. In succeeding years God called many outstanding missionaries to serve in Hong Kong.

UPDATE 2000 In order to plant churches, along with traditional methods of evangelism, missionaries used a medical clinic, kindergartens and day care centers, study centers for youth, and service centers for the elderly. Over the years, China Baptist Theological College has trained local leaders. Graduates from this school now serve in key positions: Dr. Teddy Cheng is the president of CBTC; and the first graduate, Rev. Po Wan Yeung, is ABWE's administrator for International Chinese Ministries. ABWE missionaries and local Chinese pastors have planted 33 churches in Hong Kong.

TIBET

Linguist Paul Miller brought the challenge of Tibet to ABWE. At first the board felt entering Tibet would be overextension when existing fields needed personnel. Also, because of Paul's nondenominational training, the Board recommended he approach the China Inland Mission. Unimpressed with that suggestion, Paul assured the board that he wanted to identify with ABWE. Paul and Helen Miller were accepted as ABWE missionaries and appointed to Tibet in March 1947.

The Millers decided to approach Tibet through the Yunnan Province of China and begin their language study in Sikang, Tibet.

After determining there were no language study opportunities in that area, they accepted an invitation from missionary friends to study in Darjeeling, India. The Executive Committee approved this plan, and the Millers set out for India.

Visa difficulties delayed them in Hong Kong while their baggage went on to Calcutta. They finally obtained student visas and eventually reached Darjeeling. After some time they moved to Kalimpong, located in the narrow corridor of India bordering Nepal and Bhutan. During his time in those countries Paul translated the Gospel of Mark into Bhutanese. Early in 1952 the Millers returned on furlough, confident they would return to work with the Tibetan people. That didn't happen. Unable to get visas, the Millers were stalled in North America for two more years.

INDIA

The great sub-continent of India continued to occupy the minds and hearts of the mission. The hope had been to send the Bill Reid family and the Warner sisters to Ceylon (now called Sri Lanka), but the Ceylon government refused to grant visas.

The board continued to receive applications from people who wanted to work in India. Dick and Rose Durham felt a burden for the Muslims in India. In October 1953 the board appointed the Durhams for service in India with the hope that ABWE could somehow get on the Indian government's visa approval list.

About this same time, Bessie Turnbull and Gladys MacLean, who had been working in India under the Canadian Baptist Foreign Mission Society, became unhappy with the liberalism they saw creeping into their organization. They resigned, made application to ABWE, and were accepted in October 1954. As Canadian citizens, whose country was a member of the British Commonwealth of Nations, they had no problem getting visas into India.

In 1955, Bessie Turnbull and Gladys MacLean returned to their work in India. Unable to obtain entry into India, the Durham family proceeded to Manila, and the Reids and the Warners went to Hong Kong. Also, that year, Australians Victor and Winnifred Barnard entered the picture.

EAST PAKISTAN

The Barnard family had served in Bengal, India, under the Australian Baptist Foreign Missionary Society. After 25 years, Victor resigned and accepted a pastorate in Australia. Learning about ABWE, he initiated correspondence. This led to the Barnards going to North America and meeting with the ABWE board. They were accepted as missionaries at the annual board meeting in April 1955 and appointed to India.

In 1947 India had been partitioned into the predominantly Hindu nation of India in the center, sandwiched between the West and East wings of Pakistan, formed as a homeland for Muslims. The Barnards had worked among the Muslims, and the Dick Durhams had been burdened for Muslim work in India. They were selected to conduct a survey of East Pakistan in July and August 1955. Acting upon their report, in October 1955 the board voted to enter East Pakistan.

Finally, however, the Durhams decided to continue their work in the Philippines. Since Paul and Helen Miller could not get into Tibet, they felt it was time to shift gears and join the Barnards in becoming ABWE's first missionaries to East Pakistan.

Eight

Developments on the Home Front

The year 1952 marked ABWE's 25th anniversary. For the first ten years the mission operated only in the Philippines under the ABEO name. The second decade saw the metamorphosis of ABEO into ABWE with the expansion into South America. As the second decade closed, the mission revived work in the Philippines, expanded the South American fields, and entered south China. Early in the third decade, efforts to work in Ceylon and Tibet proved unsuccessful. ABWE missionaries were able, however, to enter India, Hong Kong, and East Pakistan.

During these years, ABWE's missionary family and staff grew. Alice Hudson became the treasurer, and former missionary Jim Ker, the deputation director. Due to his wife's ill health, Jim stayed only for one year. In October 1944, Donald Moffat took over as deputation director. He and his wife, Lois, had served with Baptist Mid-Missions in Brazil for a number of years. Don was a dynamic speaker who influenced a number of individuals to become career missionaries during his ten years as deputation director. It is he who challenged students at the London Bible Institute in London, Ontario, recruiting the pioneers of what is now ABWE–Canada.

In September 1945 Mrs. Doane purchased for the mission a stately residence at 6605 Wayne Avenue in Germantown, Pennsylvania. This generous gift served as the venue for candidate classes. When the classes became too large, they were moved to the campus of the Baptist Bible College at Clarks Summit,

Pennsylvania. The Germantown property was sold in 1969 when ABWE moved from Philadelphia to Cherry Hill, New Jersey. Proceeds from the sale provided a nest egg with which to begin construction in Cherry Hill.

As the mission grew, the financial details became too much for Miss Hudson to handle. Alfred Schlicter, who lived in Germantown, had spent 18 years as a missionary with the China Inland Mission and had been treasurer of that organization. He shared ABWE's doctrinal position, and in April 1946 was appointed associate treasurer. Three years later, Rev. Schlicter suffered a heart attack and died. Ed and Marian Bomm were on furlough at that time. Ed had done a fine job as treasurer and business agent in Manila. After obtaining his agreement, the board elected him treasurer, a position he held until his retirement in 1971.

In the spring of 1947, when for health reasons they could not return to the Upper Amazon, Robert and Frances Burns were appointed as ABWE Midwestern representatives. In the fall of 1950 Paul and Kay Friederichsen returned from the Philippines. The war years had taken their toll, and the Friederichsens were unable to continue their overseas ministries. They became the Midwestern representatives and the Burnses moved back to Philadelphia. Bob Burns became assistant deputation director working with Don Moffat. Frances Burns began working in the publications department, a position she held until her retirement.

In September 1951 Rev. Donald MacKay resigned from the pastorate of Central Baptist Church in Gary, Indiana, to become the full-time vice-president of ABWE, assisting Dr. Commons in the growing administrative work. The MacKays made an extended trip to the Far East to see the work in the Philippines and Hong Kong. They also made a brief stop in Japan sizing up possible ministry opportunities for the future.

Other changes occurred in 1951. Realizing his gifts were in itinerant preaching, Don Moffat became the Southwestern representative. Bob Burns moved into the position of deputation director

25th ANNIVERSARY

The silver anniversary celebration took place on April 9, 1953, the date of the signing of the original incorporation documents. Dr. and Mrs. Raphael Thomas were unable to attend but sent their greetings, including an account of some of their early experiences in the Philippines. Eighty-four-year-old Ellen Martien journeyed to Philadelphia for the occasion. Her engaging personality and witty reminiscences contributed much to the program. Alice Drake also represented the missionaries involved in the early period. Bessie Traber and Helen Hinkley had other responsibilities that prevented their coming.

By ABWE's 25th anniversary, a feeling of confidence permeated the ranks. The mission had passed through the growing pains of adolescence and arrived at a state of maturity that bode well for the future.

The May 1952 *Message* magazine headline read: "Greatest Year in ABWE's History." The same issue mentioned that more than a half-million dollars had been given for missions and the missionary family had grown to 130 members.

Nine

New Frontiers in the Fifties

The 25th anniversary was marked by a forward look. In the October 1953 board meetings ABWE appointed 11 new missionaries and voted to enter two new fields.

JAPAN

When the Japanese emperor, Hirohito, surrendered to General Douglas MacArthur he also acknowledged publicly that he was not a god and should not be worshipped. This created a religious upheaval in Japan, leaving a spiritual vacuum that presented a great opportunity for missionary work. The General issued a call for large numbers of missionaries to work in Japan during the period of his administration.

During vice president Don MacKay's visit to Japan he had interviewed a number of missionaries to determine the neediest areas for missionary work. His findings drew attention to the southern island of Kyushu, particularly Kagoshima Prefecture. Vernon and Marian Chandler and Elaine Potter were appointed to Japan.

Prior to the Morgan's return from the Philippines to Hong Kong, the board asked if they would initiate ABWE's entry into Japan. They agreed and moved to the city of Kagoshima, secured a house, a language teacher, and started holding Bible classes. The Chandlers and Elaine Potter joined them in the fall. The next year, Paul and Vada Shook and Mary Goodson joined the team.

Soon the beginnings of a church had been established in Kagoshima and the work spread north to the towns of Hayato and Chosa. The Morgans, having fulfilled their assignment, returned to Hong Kong.

The Japanese language requires several years to learn, but the Chandlers started a work in Kobe even while attending language school. They stayed with that work until retirement. Gerald and Virginia Winters started a work in the large industrial city of Fukuoka in northwestern Kyushu.

UPDATE 2000 Ministries in Japan center around church planting using methods such as teaching conversational English, cooking classes, sports, Camp Shalom, and several outreaches to the hearing-impaired. ABWE in Japan is an ambitious team seeking to multiply church plants through friendship evangelism.

CHILE

Simultaneously, with the opening of Japan, came additional expansion in South America. This resulted from a plea for help from a group of independent Baptist churches in Chile which asked ABWE to start a Bible institute in Santiago. Ed Bomm and several ABWE missionaries from Brazil met with Chilean pastors in the summer of 1951. Mr. Bomm shared a challenging report on his return. A year later, the board asked two veteran missionaries, Ernest Olsen and Walter (Bud) Craymer, to revisit Chile. They, too, were enthusiastic about the open door, religious freedom, and unprecedented opportunity in Chile. They recommended ABWE open that field. The board acted favorably and requested that Ernest and Eleanore Olsen and Bud and Ellen Craymer transfer from Peru to Chile. Both families accepted this challenge. Margaret Bock was the first new appointee to Chile. To strengthen the new work, Bill and Ruth Hopewell transferred there from the Philippines.

New missionaries appointed to Chile included Jay and Norma

Jean Dyksterhouse, Donald and Mary Lang, Elmer and Marjorie Cassidy, Richard and Larrie Tice, Marion Schwenk, Mary Brock, Mary O'Neil, Virginia Forkell, and Virginia Allen. The work began with tent campaigns in the suburbs of Santiago. In 1955 the field council purchased property on the outskirts of Santiago, where a Bible school and two missionary dwellings were constructed.

In spite of this good start, Chile has proven to be one of ABWE's most difficult fields. An unusually large turnover of missionary personnel has kept the work from growing as much as was hoped. In recent years, however, God has sent the right combination of missionary personnel who have advanced the work immensely.

UPDATE 2000 ABWE focuses its activity in Santiago, the country's large and bustling capital. The Baptist Bible Institute and Seminary trains Chilean believers. ABWE missionaries serve on teams with Chilean Christians in the school, as well as in other areas of ministry. Widespread contact with local people is a result of the Bible correspondence courses and personal Bible studies. Many have been led to Christ and are active in their local churches. Missionary children attend pre-K through 12th grade at Santiago Christian Academy, a beautiful complex near the snowcapped Andes Mountains.

EAST PAKISTAN

Following the initial survey, the board voted in October 1955 to declare East Pakistan a new ABWE field. In 1957 Paul and Helen Miller joined Victor and Winnifred Barnard in the port city of Chittagong. Later that year, they made extensive surveys of the Chittagong Hill Tracts District bordering on Burma (now called Myanmar). Their hearts were moved with compassion as they encountered various tribes such as Murungs, Tripuras, Marmas, Chaks, and Chakmas. The goals of those pioneer missionaries were to reach these primitive tribes and to establish a base in Chittagong from where they could work among the coastal Bengali people, including Muslims, Hindus, and Buddhists.

In 1958 Gene and Elizabeth Gurganus, Mary Lou Brownell, Juanita Canfield, Miriam Morin, and Joyce Ann Wingo arrived in Chittagong. In January 1960 Jay and Eleanor Walsh joined the team.

Two deaths in the missionary family resulted in personnel changes and the establishment of a medical ministry. In January 1957 the Barnards' 14-year-old daughter, Winnifred Mary, died of peritonitis. In May 1959, Paul Miller died of polio. Recurrent illnesses affected the Barnards, and sickness forced the Gurganuses to return to the United States. The once-sizable force was reduced to four.

By 1962 the Gurganuses had returned, and meetings were started in Chittagong. Gene Gurganus opened the Bible Correspondence School (BCS) which flourishes to this day.

Winnifred Mary Barnard's death played a vital part in leading Dr. Viggo (Vic) and Joan Olsen to give their lives for medical mission work. Dr. Olsen met with the board in April 1959 and presented a paper giving his "Basic Principles of Medical/Surgical Evangelism." The board voted unanimously to adopt this policy statement, and the Olsens were appointed as medical missionaries to East Pakistan, arriving there in January 1962.

Vic and Jay entered into lengthy negotiations with the East Pakistan government, and eventually ABWE was granted a 33-year lease on 25 acres of land located in the national forest 65 miles south of Chittagong. Construction of the hospital and missionary housing began in 1963, and the Memorial Christian Hospital was dedicated and opened for service to the public in March 1966.

Satan has opposed the work in various ways, including the mysterious death of Harry Goehring in June 1965 (possibly by poison) in spite of the utmost efforts of Drs. Ralph and Lucy Ankenman, Donn Ketcham, and Vic Olsen.

The revolutionary war of 1971 gave birth to the People's Republic of Bangladesh. Parts of this story of God's protection and provision have been published in books written by Bangladesh missionaries:

- *Daktar,* by Dr. Viggo B. Olsen
- *On Duty in Bangladesh,* by Jeannie Lockerbie
- *Against All Odds,* by Jay Walsh

Those, and the following books about Bangladesh, are available through ABWE Publishing:

- *Ripe Mangoes,* by Jay Walsh (stories of Bangladeshi Christians)
- *Write the Vision,* by Jeannie Lockerbie (the founding and growth of the Literature Division)
- *It Could Happen to You,* by Dr. John Bullock (John and Tense Bullocks' call to salvation and service)
- *Bangladesh At A Glance* (an overview of the country and an introduction to customs and culture)
- *A Trip To Where?* by Kim Rosenau (a five-day series for children including the story, flashcards, and activities)

UPDATE 2000 More than 120 tribal village churches have been planted in the Chittagong Hill Tracts. In 1989, tribal Christian leaders representing 55 village churches formed the Bangladesh Tribal Association of Baptist Churches.

On the plains among the mostly non-tribal Bangladeshis, 35 churches or preaching points have been started. National leadership training is a priority, accomplished through the Baptist Bible College and personal discipleship. Camp, Bible Correspondence School, self-help handicraft programs, schools for missionary and national children, audio/visual productions, and teaching English are all vital parts of the work in Bangladesh.

Some of these ministries are carried out at Memorial Christian Hospital, which is renovating and enlarging the facility to meet the needs of a growing population.

The Literature Division in Chittagong is the largest producer of Christian literature in Bengali, the fourth most spoken language in the world. The greatest accomplishment for evangelism and church planting in the Bengali-speaking world has been the translation of the Bible into the common language of the people. Lynn Silvernale and her team produced the Standard Bengali Common Language Bible. This base has been used to produce adaptations for Muslim readers and translations into several other languages.

THE EARLY YEARS

(1927–1960)

Dr. and Mrs. Raphael Thomas

Ed and Marian Bomm, 1946

Don and Helen Hare and their evangelistic tent meetings

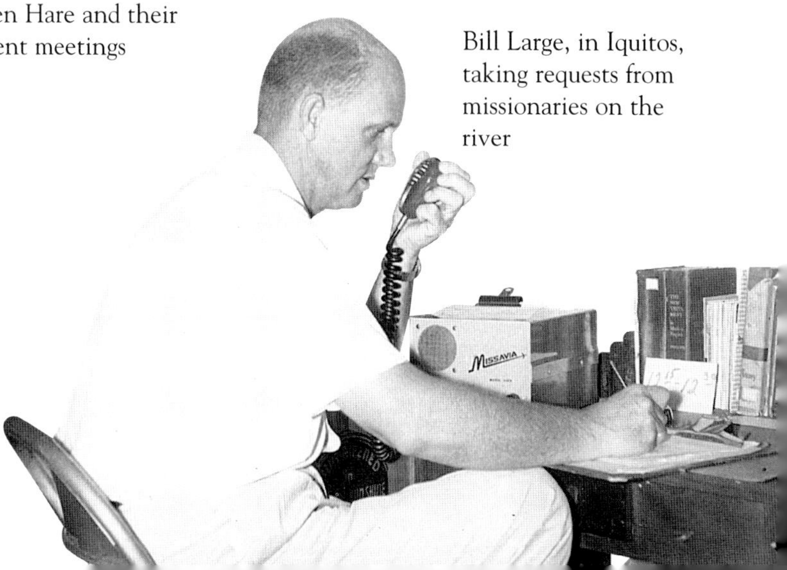

Bill Large, in Iquitos, taking requests from missionaries on the river

Above Left:
Gospel Ship, 1936

Above Right:
ABWE office, 1505 Race St., Philadelphia

Above:
Mission house in Germantown, Pa., where candidate classes were held

Left:
Mona Kemery and Ruth Woodworth in Filipina dress

Jay Morgan (back left) and Vern Chandler (back right), at first camp in Japan

Above:
Doane Baptist Bible Institute, in Iloilo

Left:
Winnifred Barnard and daughter, East Pakistan

Left:
Victor and Margaret Barnett with Dorothy and Jaymes Morgan, 1949

Below:
Bill and Elva Scherer, Upper Amazon

Left to right: Esther Yerger, Betty Traber, Mrs. Doane, Mrs. Peabody, Alice Hudson, Ruth Woodworth, and Alice Drake

Carl Matthews, Brazil

Ten

Internal Growth and Consolidation

In 1957 ABWE missionaries worked in eight countries: the Philippines, Hong Kong, Japan, East Pakistan, Brazil, Colombia, Peru, and Chile. By that time, six Bible institutes had been established for training national leadership. During the 1960's ABWE's home base was strengthened and resources were put into fortifying existing fields.

Harold & Helen Amstutz

In Dr. Common's April 1957 report, he mentioned the addition of two new staff members: Harold Amstutz, as candidate and deputation secretary, and Donald Drake, as assistant to the treasurer.

The report also mentioned that the board had established a retirement program. After studying retirement policies of various missions, Ed Bomm designed this three-pronged policy:

1. The entire ABWE family would participate in the U.S. government's Social Security program or the equivalent Canadian plan.
2. ABWE would purchase a group retirement policy to provide a nominal fixed monthly income for each retired missionary 65 years and older.

3. The mission would request the missionaries' supporting churches to continue partial support, the amount to be determined according to individual needs.

These retirement funds would be mission controlled and would care for the missionaries' health insurance, account maintenance, and ongoing ministries.

In 1956 ABWE had negotiated a contract with Blue Cross/Blue Shield for a supplemental insurance (BC/BS 65 Plus). This insurance picks up most medical or surgical expenses not covered by Medicare. The retirement and insurance programs have worked well over the years and have proven to be a great help to ABWE missionaries and their supporters.

During the 1960's efforts were also made to improve liaison between the mission office and the fields. ABWE determined early on never to center authority in any one individual. Field council chairmen, country coordinators, or executive administrators, working from the mission headquarters, were not to make unilateral policy decisions. Policies would be made by the full board or the Executive Committee of the board and relayed to the fields. To have a close relationship with the mission fields, however, a procedure was inaugurated to encourage the mission president, other home office personnel, pastors, and board members to make periodic visits to see the work firsthand and to interact with the missionaries. From the decade of the 1960's onward, a fairly close bond has been maintained between headquarters and the various fields. No system is perfect, but in the absence of field directors or a general director, this setup has enabled the board to function intelligently when confronted with problems referred to it by the field councils. The board is the final authority, but has granted field councils autonomy to run their affairs within reasonable boundaries.

ABWE–CANADA

A significant development in this decade involved the Canadian office. In 1967 the United States Internal Revenue Service notified ABWE that the Canadian treasurer could no longer issue tax deductible receipts to their donors. At the October 1968 board meeting an eight-man council was named to officially form ABWE–Canada. Five members were Canadians and three Americans. The policy was established that the five Canadians formed an Executive Committee that would meet periodically in Canada, and ABWE–Canada would always holds its annual meeting in conjunction with ABWE's annual meeting in the United States.

The following men formed the first Canadian board: Rev. Roy Lawson, chairman; Rev. David Irwin, secretary; Rev. Leander Roblin, treasurer; Rev. Vincent Trimmer, and Dr. Charles Bray. Dr. Harold Commons, Rev. Edward Bomm, and Dr. Kenneth Masteller were the Americans on that board. This official action made ABWE international in nature and also solved the tax deductible receipt problem.

Besides handling finances, however, the mission wanted a Canadian to represent ABWE in churches and colleges across Canada. Rev. Leander Roblin assumed that position in 1961. In 1975, following the death of his wife, Dorothy, Mel Cuthbert returned to Canada from Brazil. He spent five years developing ABWE–Canada, then returned to Brazil. At that time, Reg and Helen Snell came out of the pastorate to take this position. Ivor and Ruth Greenslade headed up ABWE–Canada for a short while when Ivor had to leave Brazil for health reasons.

Frank & Brenda Bale

UPDATE 2000 Since 1992, Frank and Brenda Bale, who were ABWE missionaries in Brazil and Portugal, have served as the Canadian directors. David Irwin acted as chairman of the Canadian Council for 25 years; this position is now held by Marvin Brubacher.

ABWE–Canada has 35 missionaries (including five appointees) and serves in 12 countries. The Canadian office is located at:

160 Adelaide Street, South—Suite 205
London, Ontario N5Z 3L1

Back at the headquarters in Philadelphia, additions to the office staff improved the total operation of ABWE. Ed Bomm brought in Rev. Donald Drake in 1956. Don served as assistant treasurer for seven years before resigning to complete his studies in Christian education. Rev. B. Donald Sutherland, an ABWE board member, became associate treasurer to Ed Bomm and succeeded him as treasurer when Ed retired in 1971.

With his own retirement pending, and Donald Sutherland's not too far behind, Ed Bomm felt the importance of bringing in younger men. In 1966 Robert Auffort, an accountant, was made assistant to Mr. Sutherland. The following year, William Pierson became Mr. Bomm's assistant. These two men knew each other and worked well together. After the Bomms and Sutherlands retired, Bob Auffort became accountant and associate treasurer, and Bill Pierson became treasurer.

In October 1967 the mission celebrated its 40th year in world evangelism. In those meetings ABWE reaffirmed its separatist stand toward ecumenical evangelism and its historic emphasis on soul winning and church planting. The board also set goals to give the mission specific aims. These included:

1. To pray for the mission, the home staff, and the missionaries for 40 hours during the year. This figured out to be less than seven minutes a day.
2. To work toward enrolling 40 new missionary candidates for the year.
3. To establish 40 new churches throughout the ABWE world.

4. To raise funds for the general operation of the mission in multiples of $40. Each board member would try to enlist churches to support ABWE for the sum of $40 a month.

Eleven

Advancing into New Fields

SPAIN

After many years of the Franco dictatorship, the door to Spain seemed to open at last. It had been almost impossible for missionaries to enter Spain under his rule. In October 1967 the board sent Bud Craymer, on furlough from Chile, and Bob Burns, both of whom were fluent in Spanish, to survey the situation.

The men arrived in Madrid on November 6, 1967. Their most important contact was with Dr. Jose Cardona, executive secretary of the Evangelical Defense Committee representing Protestant groups before the Spanish government. He gave reliable information about the extent of gospel ministry in the country and the probable effect of the new Spanish law on religious liberty.

The Burns/Craymer team traveled from Madrid to Segovia, Burgos, Bilbao, Pamplona, Zaragoza, Valencia, and Malaga visiting missionaries and other Christian contacts. They concluded there was not only opportunity for church planting in Spain; there was a great need for it. The population of Spain at that time was 32 million. Only about 200 of the 9,000 towns and villages had any sort of gospel testimony.

Upon receipt of their report and recommendation, the board declared Spain a new ABWE field and issued a call to prayer for personnel. The first to respond were Bill and Rosie Stoner, on furlough from Chile. The board approved the Stoners' transfer to

Spain, and they began sharing the challenge of Spain in North American churches.

Bill and Pat Hawk, from the October 1968 candidate class, were appointed. The Stoners arrived in Spain in 1968, and the Hawks joined them in 1970. They started church planting at the eastern edge of the capital city, Madrid. The Stoners later moved to Zaragoza, the center of Mary worship in Spain. Roy and Nancy Jones used children's clubs and the showing of evangelistic films to open up work in Coslada, east of Madrid. Larry and Jane Parks opened up work in Toledo, another ancient Roman Catholic stronghold.

UPDATE 2000 When the early ABWE missionaries arrived, intolerance was still rampant. Over the years, missionaries have experienced a transition into religious liberty. From a legal perspective, the opportunities to evangelize are now practically limitless. Nevertheless, the intense hold of Roman Catholicism on all spheres of Spanish life is still a power to be reckoned with. Innovative approaches, such as sports evangelism and weekday classes in crafts, English, and music open doors and make contacts for the gospel.

WEST GERMANY

The winds of expansion continued to blow in the early years of ABWE's fifth decade. Several prospective candidates manifested a concern for Germany and were authorized to make a personal survey in the summer of 1967. Rather than spearhead ABWE's entrance into that country, they decided to join another group already working there. Since no other candidates were interested, this proposed new field did not develop until much later.

VIETNAM

Vietnam lay heavily on American hearts during the military involvement there. Board member William Kuhnle, head of the

Chaplain's Commission of the General Association of Regular Baptist Churches, made a trip to investigate possibilities for missions in that country. Every contact he made was favorable. He reported that ABWE could count on the cooperation of the military in any missionary efforts.

Hopes for entering Vietnam were dashed at that time, however, when the U.S. government's "no win" policy led to a huge military defeat by the communist Viet Cong.

UPDATE 2000 By the end of the 1990's ABWE had a gateway to enter and stay in Vietnam through teaching English as a Second Language. Contacts had also been made with indigenous pastors and small house churches.

ABWE's first career missionary couple began evaluating and developing ministry opportunities in Vietnam in 1998. Later, in 1999, the board voted officially to open Vietnam as an ABWE field.

AUSTRALIA

As Larry and Jacqueline Armstrong finished their second term in the Philippines, they felt increasingly that ABWE could decrease its missionary force there and allow the nationals to carry more responsibility for reaching their own people. With this motivation the Armstrongs requested the board's permission to visit Australia in the fall of 1969. Authorization was given. The needs and opportunities in the land "down under" so impressed the Armstrongs that, when they met with the board in the fall of 1970, they requested a transfer from the Philippines to Australia. Thus, the board declared Australia a field of ABWE and assigned the Armstrongs to lead the endeavor.

Later, David and Beverly Toro asked for a transfer from Chile to Australia. The Armstrongs arrived in the fall of 1971; the Toros followed in the spring of 1972. They chose Sydney as the best place to begin.

John and Vira Baker were appointed in 1972. They planted

Berean Baptist Church in Woloongong, New South Wales. Carrel and Fern Aagard and Frank and Sophie Jenista transferred from the Philippines. With this influx of missionaries, the Australian Field Council launched the Spurgeon Baptist Bible Institute (later changed to Spurgeon Baptist Bible Theological College) to train future pastors and evangelists. Although the college ceased to exist, graduates serve in churches in New South Wales, Victoria, Northern Territories Western Australia, and in Malta and New Zealand.

UPDATE 2000 Six churches have been started in the Sydney area, and church-planting teams try new ideas, creative outreaches, and innovative ways to reach a secular population who "don't have time for religion."

Unlike the United States, Australia welcomes volunteers to teach the Bible in the public schools. Opportunities for evangelism are unlimited, yet it is estimated that only 2% of Australians have genuine faith in Christ.

The world has come to Australia. Only Israel has a higher percentage of recent immigrants. Extensive immigration has created a multi-cultural nation presenting unique challenges for cross-cultural evangelism.

Twelve

Strategic Changes at Home Base

RELOCATION OF OFFICE

For a number of reasons, mainly financial, the board felt led to consider relocating the mission. At first, they contemplated purchasing various buildings within the city of Philadelphia. None appeared adaptable to the mission's needs.

In 1968 the board appointed a committee to study the situation and make a recommendation, because by this time sufficient resources were available to purchase land and build. After investigating various sites, the committee located a place in Cherry Hill, New Jersey, across the Delaware River from Philadelphia. It consisted of 5.6 acres of land along Springdale Road and included two houses in a principally residential area. A major highway and a major interstate expressway with connections in all directions were only blocks away. The property lay immediately adjacent to the Bethel Baptist Church of Cherry Hill. Through a Christian realtor, the mission made an offer lower than the asking price. Then people prayed. The owner accepted the offer!

Plans were drawn and the news publicized. Construction started in the fall of 1970 and the move was made in the summer of 1971. Staff members were happy with the purchase of new equipment, and the entire mission family was pleased with the new facility. God provided sufficient funds over the next few years to pay off the mortgage. The Cherry Hill municipality granted tax exemption. The mission benefited greatly from the move.

CHANGE OF LEADERSHIP

At the same time as the move to Cherry Hill, a search began for a new president. Dr. Commons was to turn 65 in 1970. He had told the ABWE board that 35 years at the helm was enough. Dr. Joseph Stowell was appointed chairman of the Search Committee. The committee first took a hard and prayerful look at the existing staff. Perhaps someone in the administration could be elevated to the job. When they failed to reach a consensus, the committee looked for a candidate among the missionary personnel. Once again they came up empty-handed, and the chairman suggested that his frustrated committee be dissolved and a new one appointed. But Dr. Commons insisted that no better committee could be found, and challenged them to a fresh start.

By the fall of 1970 Dr. Commons had turned 65. He agreed to serve until after the annual meeting in the spring of 1971, but that would be it. When he retired he wanted to be totally out of the picture and give the new president a free hand to build his own administrative team.

The search continued until Wendell W. Kempton came into the picture. The spring 1971 *Message* magazine records,

> Almost out of a clear blue sky one man was suggested who, upon close examination, seemed to possess all the qualifications. Youth, education, culture, spiritual experience, vitality, vision, missionary enthusiasm, soul-winning burden, winsome and pleasing personality, theological acumen coupled with solid Baptist and separatist convictions, platform presence, teaching and preaching ability—you name it, this man had it!

The committee decided to phone Wendell Kempton to see if he would be available for an interview. He agreed to drop everything and come to Philadelphia.

On February 9, 1971, the board interviewed Wendell and his

wife, Karolyn. After the unanimous recommendation by the Search Committee, the board voted unanimously to call Wendell Kempton to become the third president of the ABWE.

Following many days of prayer for God's leading, Wendell Kempton resigned from his responsibilities at the Baptist Bible Seminary in Clark's Summit, Pennsylvania, where he had been since 1961, and accepted the presidency.

Within a year of his joining ABWE, the Grand Rapids Baptist College and Seminary awarded him an honorary Doctor of Divinity degree.

A smooth transition took place during late spring and early summer of 1971. The Kempton family moved into one of the two houses on the Cherry Hill property and Wendell Kempton became the first to occupy the president's office in the new international headquarters at Cherry Hill, New Jersey.

Ed Bomm officially retired that fall, but continued as a part-time consultant to the president.

After getting a feel of things at the home base, Dr. Kempton visited the Far East in 1972, followed by a trip to South America in 1974. This allowed him to meet the missionaries and see the work firsthand.

Thirteen

ABWE's Ever-Expanding World

ABWE had no work in Africa. Up until this time, when candidates asked about serving in Africa, they were directed to mission agencies such as Baptist Mid-Missions or Evangelical Baptist Missions. As ABWE entered its fifth decade, the new administration realized once more that "the field is the world," and many countries still need the gospel message.

In July 1972 the board voted unanimously to enter Africa. An African Research Committee composed of Harold Amstutz, board member Robert Reese, and Dallas and Kay Washer investigated the needs and possibilities in Togo and the island of Mauritius.

TOGO, WEST AFRICA

The survey team found an open door and a great need in Togo. Upon hearing their report, the board voted in January 1973 to open Togo as a new ABWE field. From the July 1973 candidate classes, the board appointed four couples to Togo: Dallas and Kay Washer, David and Elwanda Fields, Tim and Esther Neufeld, and James and Carole Plunkitt. They planned to establish headquarters in the capital city of Lomé located on the coast. They would begin their work in French, the governmental and trade language.

The Dallas Washers arrived in early 1974, rented a home in Lomé, and initiated the work. The Fields joined them soon after. Both of these couples went to Togo with many years of missionary experience in other African countries. Within three weeks of their arrival, the Fields began weeknight Bible studies in their home in Bè. It was easy to get a hearing because people were curious. They were also suspicious of the missionaries, and decisions for salvation were few and far between. The Fields' house, where the meetings took place, was only two lots away from a witch doctor's compound. Drums pounded from his yard and a fresh, bloody, sacrificial chicken hung constantly over the doorway.

In August 1975, Dal and Kay Washer's son Ron and his wife, Ann, were appointed to Togo. The following year Ron's brother Dennis and his wife, Diane, were added. A third brother, Terry, and his wife, Sandy, joined the team in 1981. By the time of ABWE's 50th anniversary, missionaries in Togo were talking of establishing a small hospital and an aviation ministry.

From the beginning, Satan opposed the missionary efforts. A turning point in the work came in 1979 when, after two unsuccessful attempts, a chapel was established at Bè. The nationals started showing interest in the Word of God and a willingness to submit to its teaching. In 1983 the *l'Eglise Baptiste de Bè* became independent, and has since started other churches. The church building stands two lots away from the Fields' house—on the very spot where the witch doctor once beat his drums and sacrificed his chickens.

Dal and Kay Washer moved inland in 1976 and started the second major work in Kpalimé. In addition to starting village churches, they founded the Blind Center *(Centre des Aveugles)*. This has kept ABWE in the good graces of the government and, at the same time, provided opportunities to win many people to Christ. At the 25th anniversary of the Blind Center, held in October 1999, Kay Washer stated, "As the government ministers saw our students' achievements, they granted permission for them to write their six-year exam, then to attend college and university."

The Karolyn Kempton Memorial Christian Hospital opened its doors in July 1985. Since then, thousands of Togolese have come for health care and have heard the gospel message. July 10, 1999 marked graduation day for the first class in the nurses' training program. The *Institut de Formation D'Infirmiers* trains national men and women as skilled professional nurses who can give compassionate care as well as witness for Christ.

The airstrip was completed by a six-man team in just six weeks in 1995. It proved its worth when Kay Washer fell in May 1996, breaking many bones. She was airlifted from the hospital to the airport in Lomé.

UPDATE 2000 Since 1974 over 40 churches have been established, half of which are independent and self-supporting. Four branches of local Bible institutes operate with the goal of training national pastors. Six hours north of Lomé, in the mushrooming city of Kara, a newly formed church is branching out into several areas. Local churches have started Christian schools to better train children. Missionaries are also concerned about the ever-growing influence of Islam thoughout Togo. The Communications Resource Center, located on the hospital property, provides a multifaceted reading room in which tracts, booklets, books, and cassettes in many of Togo's languages are available.

MAURITIUS

Mauritius was included in the initial survey because of candidates interested in working on that island in the Indian Ocean. The survey was favorable, the need for missionary work evident, and the board voted to enter. This proved impossible, however, because the British government refused to grant visas to any new missionary agencies. To date, ABWE has been unable to be a part of spreading the gospel in this area.

PARAGUAY

Michael and Elaine McCubbins came to ABWE after serving one term in Paraguay with another mission. They were appointed to Peru because ABWE had no work in Paraguay. At that time, Robert and Lynne Trout, furloughing missionaries from coastal Peru, became interested in Paraguay and eventually requested a transfer.

In June 1974 the board sent a survey team consisting of Bob Trout, Michael McCubbins, Dr. Warren Bibighaus, and Bill Hopewell to look into the missionary situation there. In spite of cold, wintertime conditions, the team visited the capital city of Asunción, and other strategic locations. Also, learning that Asunción was one of South America's fastest growing cities, the survey team recommended that ABWE open the field of Paraguay.

The board voted to enter Paraguay, and appointed the Trout and McCubbins families to this new field. The Trouts arrived in the fall of 1974, joined soon afterward by the McCubbinses. Following months of door-to-door visitation and tract distribution, the first work was started in a suburb of Asunción called Stroessner. On September 28, 1975, this new work held its first baptismal service in the Paraguay River. A preaching point was started in Lambaré and other suburbs.

Many towns and cities are situated off dirt roads, often closed by rains. God answered that problem by supplying ABWE's first plane and airborne church planter in 1980. The aviation ministry begun by Dale Fogg opened up Villa del Rosario, a population center 30 air miles from Asunción.

In 1976, the first classes of the Maranatha Baptist Bible Institute and Seminary were begun using programmed materials (TEE). This was later expanded to use conventional teaching methods in the preparation of leaders for the ministry.

UPDATE 2000 With a large percentage of the population under 30, emphasis is being placed on children and youth. Camp Cavaju has been developed primarily to reach young people. On that same property is the Baptist Pastors Training Center, geared to train national workers from the interior for full-time ministry. As part of their church-planting work, Kevin and Cynthia Reilly use *Fuente de Luz*, the Source of Light Bible Correspondence School. This is an individual Bible study program designed for evangelism and discipleship.

ABWE–USA 1976

For years people asked why ABWE did not have a church-planting program for the United States. The response was that other mission agencies were already targeting the United States and ABWE felt responsible for other parts of the world. Over time, the thinking of the board and the administration gradually changed. Missionaries returning from foreign ministries who, for various reasons, could not return were often interested in staying with ABWE in a state-side ministry.

Impressed afresh that reaching our "Jerusalem" was a vital part of the Great Commission of our Lord, the board voted to open the United States as an approved field for missionary ministry. Wendell Kempton, with the board's approval, was given the challenge to find a man to head up this new aspect of ABWE's evangelism and church-planting ministry. He found him on ABWE's own board. Rev. Floyd Davis, a pastor with 30 years of church-planting, pastoral, and leadership experience, became the choice for director of missions–USA. The board called him to join ABWE on a full-time basis. Floyd Davis tells of sitting on the platform at the GARBC conference in 1976 when Dr. Ernest Pickering read a resolution containing these words: ". . . we resolve 'to spread the good news of Christ's death, resurrection, and saving grace, both in our own beloved United States and in other countries of the world.'" Those words confirmed the call for Floyd and Gayle Davis. He served faithfully until his battle with cancer which claimed his life on July 4, 1982.

By ABWE's 50th anniversary in 1977–78 the Missions–USA project was well under way. An internship program was instituted to train home missionaries by assigning them to work with experienced pastors. This program greatly enhanced their effectiveness in church planting. Several missionaries who had served overseas came into the Missions–USA program. Three new churches were planted within the first two years.

UPDATE 2000 Chapter 17 brings the account up to date.

Fourteen

Organizational Structure—and a Jubilee

During the first five years of his administration, Wendell Kempton made no changes in the administrative staff. He wanted to observe, study, and think his way through the organizational and administrative problems of a growing missionary family. He soon realized that the president could no longer handle correspondence with all the fields and care for the myriad details which daily crossed his desk. He also wanted more freedom to minister in the churches, to represent the mission in conferences and seminars, and to travel to the fields. God had given him a special gift in the area of public relations, and he wanted to use it.

Expansion into new countries called for greater travel in order to maintain liaison among the missionaries, ABWE headquarters, and the supporting constituency. The president saw the need to surround himself with veteran missionaries. With board approval, he called the following men to be part of the administrative team.

Russell E. Ebersole, Jr.

Russ & Nancy Ebersole

Russ and Gene Ebersole were appointed to the Philippines in 1953. Gene had grown up in the Philippines and, with her parents, Henry and Gladys DeVries, had spent the war years in a prison camp. Russ and Gene served as church planters in Malaybalay. In 1962, Russ was appointed as missionary-at-large for the Philippines with its five sub-field councils. Early in 1964, Dr. Link Nelson diagnosed Gene as having cancer, and the Ebersoles returned to the United States. Gene died in November 1964. While caring for his five children, Russ served as an administrative assistant at the ABWE office.

Part of his duties involved meeting with missionaries in North America. One such meeting was providential. During a trip to Indiana, Russ met Nancy Goehring. She and her husband, Harry, had gone to East Pakistan in 1963, where Harry intended to translate the Bible into the languages of the tribal people. Harry died suddenly on June 15, 1965. When Russ met Nancy, she was furthering her education and caring for her three small children. God led them together and they were married in 1969.

Russ was the first of the administrators Dr. Kempton appointed. In 1977, he became the executive administrator for the Far East. The Ebersoles returned to the Philippines and traveled to the various fields for a number of years. Returning to the United States, Russ continued as executive administrator for the Far East until 1995.

William Hopewell, Jr.

Bill and Ruth Hopewell joined ABWE in 1947 and were assigned to church planting in the Philippines. The Hopewells transferred to the newly opened field of Chile in 1953. They took an eleven-year leave of absence to teach at Baptist Bible Seminary in Johnson City, New York.

Bill & Ruth Hopewell

In August 1968, the Hopewells returned to ABWE when Bill was appointed to work in the deputation department. Later, in 1977, he became the executive administrator for South America, Europe, and Africa.

William T. Commons

William & Sharon Commons

Harold Amstutz felt the wisdom of bringing in a younger man to supervise the candidate program. He was appointed as the executive research administrator, and the search began to find a new director of missionary recruitment.

Bill Commons, son of ABWE's president emeritus, Dr. Harold Commons, was chosen. Bill and Sharon Commons were appointed as ABWE missionaries to Hong Kong in 1965. After years of fruitful church planting, in April 1980 they accepted the position of director of enlistment, and the challenge to conduct the mission's candidate program.

Organizational Structure

Throughout the 1970's, President Kempton felt the wheel concept best described ABWE's organizational flow. In his mind, the coordination of communication between the board and the fields seemed to radiate like the spokes of a wheel, to and from the board through the president and the appointed regional administrators.

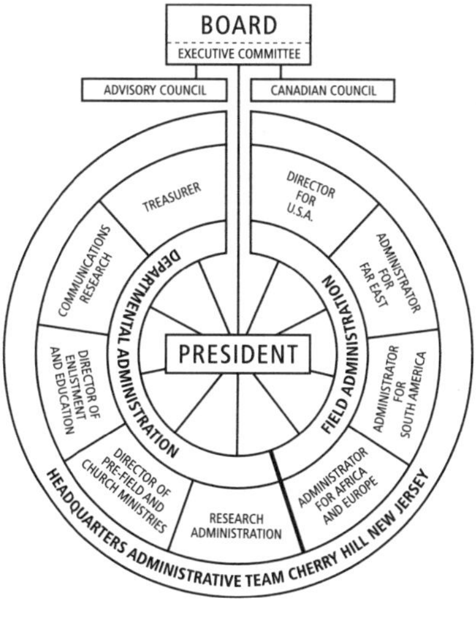

Other Additions to the Headquarters Staff

Observing the need for enriching the spiritual lives of the growing missionary family, Wendell chose Dr. J. Don Jennings as the international director of enrichment and evangelism. Don resigned the pastorate of Calvary Baptist Church, of Ypsilanti, Michigan, and began his duties at ABWE in November of 1974. His legacy is ABWE's annual Missionary Enrichment (ME) Conference.

In light of Bob Burns' impending retirement, Carl Brandon, a specialist in cinematography from Bob Jones University, became editor of the *Message* and director of communications in April 1975. Neville Chin, also a cinematography specialist, was selected from the 1977 candidate class to assist Carl Brandon.

Several veteran missionaries became or continued as ABWE representatives in various parts of North America: Mel Cuthbert, Canada; Frank Hartwig, Midwest USA; and Gene Gurganus in Southeastern USA. Retirees Victor Barnett, Paul Friederichsen, Leander Roblin, and Bill Scherer also represented the mission.

GOLDEN JUBILEE

The board set aside 1977–78 as ABWE's golden jubilee year. More than 400 people attended the anniversary banquet at the Hyatt House in Cherry Hill, New Jersey. Director of communications Carl Brandon produced an audiovisual program of the history of the mission. He also prepared a 50th anniversary issue of the *Message* in which President Kempton wrote the following, under the heading "Seedtime and Harvest":

> Years have turned into centuries since God said, '*I will never again curse the ground for man's account . . . so long as earth remains, seedtime and harvest, cold and heat, summer and winter, day and night shall not fail.*'
>
> This time-tested promise portrays the faithfulness of God to ABWE throughout its 50 years of sowing and reaping. God has faithfully given an ever-increasing harvest.

One man, Dr. Raphael Thomas, sold out to God and dedicated to evangelism, dared to reject the encroachment of liberalism and institutionalism sterilizing the missions of his day. In 1927, together with a small band of equally concerned servants of God, Dr. Thomas formed the ABEO. From this small but vigorous beginning in the Philippines, the mission, now known as ABWE, has grown to a spiritual army of over 500 missionaries laboring in 14 countries on six continents.

Rejoice with us in this ABWE's golden anniversary year. God has been faithful, abounding in grace and abundant in mercy to us and our beloved family of loyal friends. "Great things He hath done!"

Summarizing the history and growth of ABWE's first 50 years, we have much for which to be humble and thankful. I think of Mrs. Peabody and her leadership in the early days and Mrs. Doane's dedication and faithful stewardship. We are grateful to the little band of missionaries who launched ABWE in protest against liberalism and compromise.

We are grateful to the host of donors who play a major role in our worldwide outreach and especially for the 3,000 churches who support ABWE and its missionaries.

We are grateful to our wonderful family of missionaries, now numbering 500, for their faithfulness to the Great Commission.

We are grateful for the host of prayer warriors who uphold the ABWE enterprise in prayer before the Lord and for the faithful, hardworking, office staff without whom this mission could not function. But, most of all we are grateful to Him who loved and gave Himself for us and bade us to go into all the world to make known the good news of God's salvation to every creature.

It will be a great day when we see John's vision in Revelation 7:9–10 fulfilled:

After this I beheld, and, lo, a great multitude, which no man could number, of all nations, and kindreds, and people, and tongues, stood before the throne, and before the Lamb, clothed with white robes, and palms in their hands; and cried with a loud voice saying, Salvation to our God which sitteth upon the throne, and unto the Lamb.

Fifteen

Five New Fields

ARGENTINA

The headline in the January 1978 issue of the *Message* magazine read, "ABWE to Enter Argentina." The board's decision to enter this Latin American country came by way of an invitation from a youth worker in Buenos Aires which captured the attention of two experienced ABWE missionary couples.

The Greenslades had worked in the Upper Amazon region for 20 years. The Bible institute had been nationalized and many churches established in Iquitos and surrounding areas. They felt it was time to move on. Ivor and Ruth Greenslade and Jim and Sharon Evans had been praying for an opportunity to open work in Argentina. In less than a year after the board's decision, the two couples were in Argentina developing the "Team Concept of Church Planting."

God had been preparing hearts for their coming. Two women had moved into the part of Buenos Aires where the ABWE work was about to begin. They had prayed that God would open a church in that area. Soon after the missionaries' arrival, God called four Argentinian men to help in evangelism. They went door-to-door giving out tracts in 20,000 homes, and witnessed openly. Soon more than 20 new believers began coming for discipleship. The group realized they would need space for people to meet. The missionaries began negotiations to purchase a theater building that had been up for sale for over five years. Before negotiations were complete, the owner put up a sign, "Sold to the Baptist Church." People walking by asked when the church met.

Since the early days of ABWE's involvement in Argentina, missionaries and national Christian leaders have teamed up to implement a program to multiply churches in and around Buenos Aires, where over one-third of the country's population lives.

UPDATE 2000 The training of nationals holds a high priority. Argentine youth respond beautifully to the challenge of education and opportunities for leadership in an indigenous church ministry. Missionaries and local people have formed a team now engaged in evangelism, discipleship, and church planting. The prayer is that the churches in Buenos Aires will be a center from which teams can be sent to neighboring countries.

THE GAMBIA

The Gambia, one of Africa's smallest countries, is located on the Atlantic coast near the western tip of Africa. The Gambia is the native country of Junta Kinte, the great, great grandfather of Alex Haley, author of *Roots*. His native village, characterized by beautiful vegetation, is located on the north bank of the Gambia River, a few miles from the ABWE mission station of Ndungu Kebbeh. The Gambia, a predominantly Muslim country, is dominated by three West African tribes: Wolof, Mandika, and Fula.

After five terms in the Niger Republic, political upheaval forced Melvin and Ruby Pittman to leave that country. They were appointed by ABWE in 1978 and arrived in The Gambia following a survey of the country. In August 1979, they settled in the capital, Banjul, and began with evangelistic and clinic ministries on the north bank of the Gambia River. They were joined in the 1980's by nurse Ruth Wood, Dr. Wayne and Noeline Robilliard, and literacy program director Debbie Newsome. Many short-term missionaries also assisted the work in The Gambia in the early days. During 1988, the Gambia Expansion Project of the original clinic and homes resulted in much-needed new facilities. Ruth Wood's former pastor, Ralph Gruenberg, used his training as a civil engineer to head up that project. He thanked God for four "providentially balanced" teams of volunteers (65 people from 19 churches) who constructed a new multi-room clinic, additional missionary residences, and turned the former clinic into the literacy center. On March 6, 1989, the *Ndungu Kebbeh Medical and Literacy Centres* were dedicated.

UPDATE 2000 During the 1990's a vibrant team of career missionaries was formed. Current ministries in this restricted-access country include literacy, medicine, and government liaison. Nursery school, literacy classes, literature production and distribution, and a library contribute to creating interest in and knowledge of the Gospel. Chronological Bible studies are held for any who want to learn. ABWE missionaries in The Gambia are committed to follow a strategy to reach metropolitan Banjul and the tribal villages along the north bank of the Gambia River.

PORTUGAL

Another cry for help drew ABWE's attention to Europe. Christian leaders asked for help in teaching their converts, but looked in vain for independent Baptist churches. Mel and Romilda Cuthbert, veteran missionaries to Brazil, where Portuguese is spoken, were assigned to survey Portugal in 1978. After seeing areas completely void of any evangelical witness, they returned saying, "Portugal, this is your day."

God used their report to direct two missionary couples to transfer from their fields to open Portugal for ABWE work: David and Evelyn Southwell, from Brazil, and James and Carole Plunkitt, from Togo. In 1981, they launched the Portugal 20/20 Plan, which included the following points:

- A commitment to the principle of establishing 20 churches in 20 years.

- A church lot bank program, by which a church is started on a site purchased by ABWE.
- A church accepting that grant becomes responsible to purchase, at a later date, another site on which another church will be established.
- Each church is taught from the beginning the principle of reproduction; both the original church and the daughter church are expected to start a new church.

By 1993, nine churches had been started, the missionary community had grown, a school for missionary children had been established, and local people were in training as pastors, evangelists, and teachers.

UPDATE 2000 With the plan established and the goals clear, it became necessary to establish a focal point from which the ministry can advance into many communities that have no testimony of Christ. Thus, the concept of the Lisbon Training Center (LTC) was born. In October 1996, construction began on this multipurpose facility. February 1997 saw the first wave of volunteer builders. Over the next two years, more than 200 people contributed their time, sweat, and finances. The center consists of two three-story buildings connected by a large verandah. The building houses the Greater Lisbon Academy (an MK school) and a 150-seat auditorium. The second building contains dormitories, offices, and guest rooms.

The missionaries in Portugal desire that this center be used for training pastors, evangelizing children, and encouraging Portuguese Christians.

NORWAY

Norway, land of fjords and fishermen, beckoned ABWE to take another step on the European continent. A Canadian couple, James and Ruth Turpin, had already been involved in youth work in Norway when they applied to ABWE. Their interest in returning to work in Norway prompted the ABWE board to send the Turpins, Bill Hopewell, and Will Davis to survey the land. They brought back the report that at birth every citizen is accepted into the state church, but only about 2% of the population attends church. They commented, "It appears that while there is organized religion, the people are starving spiritually." The board voted to open Norway as a field of ABWE, realizing full well that this would be a difficult place in which to plant a gospel witness.

Jim and Ruth Turpin and Joe and Mary Massey, who transferred from Bangladesh, began their work in 1981 in the suburban housing development of Skjetten, which is about 13 miles from the center of Oslo, the nation's capital. By Easter Sunday 1984, a public meeting hall had been secured and worship services and Sunday school started. The church was formally organized as an independent Baptist church in 1988.

In 1985 Jack and Marilyn Slough began serving in the Free International Baptist Church. The church was formed out of a need to reach internationals in the Oslo area. Embassy personnel, university students, business people, and refugees from various places—up to 90 countries at latest count—attend the services which are conducted in English, the only language common to such a diverse group.

UPDATE 2000 The great challenges in Norway today are secularism, materialism, religious indifference, relativism, and nominal church membership. Friendship evangelism, one-on-one Bible studies, and meeting people's needs are among the methods used to make contacts. Visiting and speaking at a maximum security prison is included in Don and Gypsy Paulson's schedule as they work with Tom and Kristi VandenBerg in a new church plant on the east side of Oslo.

SOUTH AFRICA

The Republic of South Africa is often called the "Rainbow Nation," because of the mosaic of people living there. Originally, Bushmen and Hottentots roamed in and around the Cape of Good Hope. Their progressive assimilation with Negroid and East Indian slaves, white soldiers and sailors, and officials created a new ethnic group known as *Coloureds*. Dutch settlers (later known as Afrikaners) arrived in 1652, followed by English pioneers. They created a powerful *White* community. About a century after the establishment of the Cape settlement, Zulu and Xhosa tribes migrated south, creating the *Black* community. At the beginning of the 20th century, Asian workers were taken from their homes to work the sugar cane fields in Natal. They were the forerunners of the large *Indian* population.

After working in Rhodesia (now Zimbabwe) for six years, Marc and Judie Blackwell were looking for a Baptist mission agency with a team approach to church planting. They applied, and were appointed by ABWE in July 1980. During candidate class the Blackwells met Dale and Karen Marshfield, who were interested in working in South Africa. That October, a team, made up of board member Bill Parmerlee, Bill Hopewell, and Marc Blackwell surveyed South Africa. They reported that although some fine mission agencies were working in South Africa, vast areas in the large cities had no gospel witness. In the November meeting, the board voted to make South Africa ABWE's 19th mission field.

The cities of Cape Town and Durban captured the attention of the first two missionary couples. They established four principles as the strategy by which they would operate:

1. That church planting must give priority to training both pastors and lay leadership.
2. That church planting must instill a concern for and a practical commitment to establishing branch works.

3. That church planting must lead to home mission ministries staffed by trained South African workers and financed by South African churches.
4. That church planting by ABWE missionaries would be planned as part of a national strategy.

The Blackwells arrived in Westville, an area in Durban, in January 1981. After their work of surveying, evangelism, and discipleship, they opened the Church Ministries Institute. The first pastoral-trainee couple, Henry and Shirley Davis, continue to this day as senior pastor of a thriving Baptist church. When the Marshfields arrived in 1982, they joined the Davises in a team church-planting relationship.

In 1987, the Blackwells began work in Cape Town, where they established a Church Ministries Institute and effective church planting.

UPDATE 2000 From its beginnings in 1982, the team in Durban, including missionaries and South Africans, has established nine churches, a Bible college granting baccalaureate degrees, and a graduate training program.

Today in Cape Town, there are four active congregations meeting in beautiful buildings with new church plants in view.

Sixteen

Following the Leader

After his first five years at the helm, Wendell Kempton began making policy changes and additions to the staff that would set the stage for the rest of his presidency. As ABWE entered the decade of the 1980's, he led the charge for extension and growth. New ideas, surprises, and a passion for expansion permeated his administration. In his first report of the 1980's he took time to look into the rearview mirror. "Any organization that has successfully survived for 50 years has qualities worthy of note," he said. He reviewed that ABWE was an organization built upon strong leadership and one that has, in spite of periodic trials, experienced God's sovereign goodness and mercy. He then emphasized a most important point: "ABWE is an organization that is composed of a *team* of men and women with loyalty and dedication to the original objectives of the mission."

The following were concerns the president faced at the beginning of the 1980's:

- how to find the right kind of missionaries;
- how to improve their pre-field ministries to get them on the field more quickly; and
- how to improve language learning once they were there.

To find the right kind of missionaries, Wendell Kempton proposed that the Missionary Enlistment Department examine both the heart and the head of missionary candidates. Education and experience are important, but so is attitude, motivation, and good common sense. The president realized missionaries needed to be suited for the long haul.

Regarding pre-field ministry, he felt that this should be better monitored and a certain number of months allocated for raising support in order to save churches thousands of dollars. The president wanted to be more sensitive to pastors and churches in the areas of inflation and missionary support. He felt strongly that the cost of missions in both time and money needed to be cut.

Perhaps his greatest concern was for missionaries to accelerate their competency and use of the national languages. He stated, "To become fluent in the language should be the goal of every cross-cultural ABWE missionary. Language fluency not only greatly increases effectiveness in witnessing and preaching, it also contributes significantly to longevity in missionary service."

Dr. Kempton also felt it might be necessary to restructure field administration, to think about the future growth and even relocation of the mission, and to expand ABWE's work worldwide.

He presented a challenge to think about the field council concept, asking, "Is there a better or another way of administration?" He kept an open mind to change if that would enhance and improve the work.

By the end of the first decade of the Kempton presidency (1971–1981) much development could be seen:

- the ABWE family had grown from 350 to 587;
- office staff had grown from 21 to 26;
- income had risen from $2.7 million to more than $8 million annually;
- the number of countries where ABWE served had increased from 11 to 19;
- a new administrative structure involving the wheel concept had been inaugurated;
- a research department had been created;

- the accounting areas had been fully computerized;
- an estate-planning department had been created.

The office staff and missionary family was growing. Because of this, the president appointed a building committee to study whether or not to do more building on the Cherry Hill property or move to a new location. Corporate goals, including the advance of evangelism and church planting, set the course for the future decade.

Throughout the 1980's Wendell Kempton implemented the innovations and changes he often verbalized. While change threatens some and challenges others, he elicited enthusiastic support from the ABWE family. Growth in field and headquarters personnel signaled the need for change in the ABWE administration. This began to happen in 1981. The president saw the need to have experienced missionaries administer the various regions of ABWE's world. He also brought in additional staff to share the workload.

NEW PERSONNEL

Executive Administrators

By 1982 William Hopewell's work as Administrator for South America, Europe, and Africa exceeded what one man could do. The board divided the work by appointing Arthur M. Cavey as executive administrator for South America. This strategic move not only gave relief to Dr. Hopewell but greatly improved ABWE's administrative goals. Art and Joyce Cavey had served in São Paulo, Brazil, for over 30 years and were highly qualified for this new post.

In 1986 William J. Hopewell, having faithfully served as executive administrator for Europe and Africa, indicated his desire to retire to a less demanding schedule. The board selected Jesse G. Eaton to take his place. Jess and Joyce served as church-planting pastor in Fort Wayne, Indiana, for five years, then 17 years as

ABWE missionaries in Bangladesh. Upon their return to the United States, they spent five years on the faculty of the Baptist Bible Seminary of Pennsylvania. Jess began his administrative duties at ABWE in January 1987.

Communications Department

Carl Brandon, an expert in films and videos, came to ABWE in 1975 to upgrade the communications department. Veteran missionary Robert Henry, uncertain about returning to Hong Kong for health reasons, expressed interest in developing a media center for the missionaries. His goal, when he began in September 1980, was to assist missionaries to more effectively communicate missions to the churches. In time, Bob became the media center coordinator, while Carl emphasized the development of films during his time at ABWE. He resigned in 1988.

Publications

Harold Amstutz was given the temporary assignment as administrator of the publications side of the communications department in 1985. Neville Chin became the editor of the *Message* magazine and assisted in preparing other publications. In 1988 Frank Hartwig took over the publications department. He and his wife, Nancy, had served as church planters in Davao, in the Philippines. His experience as a missionary, an ABWE representative, teacher, and writer suited him for the position.

Mission Relations

In June 1989 E. C. Haskell came to ABWE to fill the post of executive administrator of mission relations. E. C.'s main thrust was to communicate missions in general, and the work of ABWE in particular, to pastors, Bible college and seminary students, and the Christian public. The three departments under his purview are publications, media, and church relations. He also serves as the personnel director and special assistant to the president.

Pre-Field and Church Ministries

Wendell Kempton gave his attention to two major concerns: missionary appointees and supporting churches. At the December 1982 Executive Committee meetings, Mel Cuthbert was appointed as director of pre-field and church ministries. Mel's relationship with ABWE stretched back to 1952, when he was appointed to São Paulo, Brazil. His new responsibility was to assist missionaries from the time of their appointment until they obtained visas and were ready to depart for their fields of service. Mel and his wife, Romilda, were also responsible for assisting pastors and churches in setting up missionary conferences, and in developing and strengthening church relations. Under Mel's tenure of service the term "deputation" became "pre-field ministry" and "furlough" became "furlough ministry."

ABWE–USA

Dr. Kempton did not plan this personnel change. God did. On July 4, 1982, Floyd Davis, director of ABWE–USA, went to heaven, free at last from the cancer that plagued him. At Floyd's funeral Wendell Kempton said about him, "He had the hands of a carpenter, the heart of a servant, the mind of an administrator, and the will of a conqueror."

Floyd Davis

Through vigilant prayer, the ABWE leadership sought the will of God in finding a successor to Floyd Davis. Norman and Evelyn Nicklas were on furlough from Brazil at the time. Norm later testified that as he heard about Floyd's home-going he felt the Holy Spirit's tug to consider taking up that ministry if the Lord should so direct. In their three terms in Brazil, Norm and Evelyn successfully started four churches. They knew the joys and struggles of planting churches. Several months later, when President Kempton approached Norm about heading up ABWE–USA, he accepted.

Evangelism and Church Growth

Throughout the 1980's the president selected people for full-time administration. In 1986 the board approved Dr. Daniel Gelatt to serve as ABWE's international administrator of evangelism and church growth, a position previously held for nine years by Dr. J. Don Jennings. Dan Gelatt resigned a successful pastoral ministry in Elkhart, Indiana, to serve in this capacity. He was born of missionary parents and served in the pastorate for more than 30 years. In his new ministry, he was to promote evangelism and church growth throughout the ABWE world.

Singles Ministries

Mary Lou Brownell's furlough from Bangladesh coincided with the growing need for someone to head a department to serve ABWE's single missionaries. In April 1986 the board approved her appointment as executive coordinator of singles ministries. After having served in Bangladesh for 30 years, Mary Lou began her new ministry on October 1, 1986. Her duties included encouraging, counseling, and assisting the nearly 100 single women serving in ABWE.

Information Systems

When ABWE's computer system became obsolete, a new IBM system was purchased to replace Basic Four. The time had come to broaden the use of the hardware from a simple centralized data-processing group to a decentralized mode to include word processing. The Lord led Paul J. Sturgis to ABWE in October 1986 to direct these changes. His experience and his love for the Lord and world missions fitted him for the responsibilities that would fall upon his shoulders in future years.

New Vice-President

At the January 1986 board meeting, the announcement was made of the appointment of Rev. Will Davis—who had served for

15 years on the ABWE board—to succeed Dr. Joseph Stowell as vice-president of ABWE. Dr. Stowell became vice-president emeritus, continuing to serve on the board and as an ABWE international representative.

Enlistment

The president's next decision provided help for the Enlistment Department. The demands of traveling to colleges and seminaries to speak and recruit new personnel required the energies of more than one person. During the October 1987 board meetings Donald Trott was appointed as co-director of enlistment and education, to serve with Bill Commons. Don and Ruth Trott came to ABWE after having served one term as ABWE missionaries to Hong Kong and 14 years at the Baptist Bible College in Clarks Summit, Pennsylvania.

ADMINISTRATIVE CHANGES

By the end of 1986 the mission family and office staff had grown to the extent that the wheel concept of administration, which had worked well in the 1970's, became obsolete. Wendell Kempton established the President's Action Committee (PAC). It started as a four-man committee composed of Art Cavey, Mel Cuthbert, Harold Amstutz, and Russ Ebersole, with Bill Pierson, Bill Commons, and Wendell Kempton as ex-officio members.

Art & Joyce Cavey

Mel & Romilda Cuthbert

Dr. Kempton explained, "Under my administration we lived with some sensitive issues and have inherited some problems which, in my judgment, could retard and cripple the ongoing effectiveness of the task God has called us to do." He listed 24 critical areas to be researched, among which were evangelism and church planting, administrative governance, field council philosophy, service to churches and missionaries, enlistment of new missionaries, and ways to minister more effectively to the missionary children.

The President's Action Committee worked hard for the next three years. Then, in 1989, the name and focus of PAC was changed from the President's Action Committee to the President's Administrative Committee.

In the April 1989 board meetings, Wendell Kempton said, "By 1986 I knew our future administration direction. It was then time to communicate and prepare our mission, from the top down, for this change."

The PAC finalized the following organizational flow chart and gained the board's approval in time for it to be included in the revised edition of ABWE's *Principles and Practices*. [Copies are available through the ABWE Publications Department.]

ABWE HEADQUARTERS ADMINISTRATIVE CHART

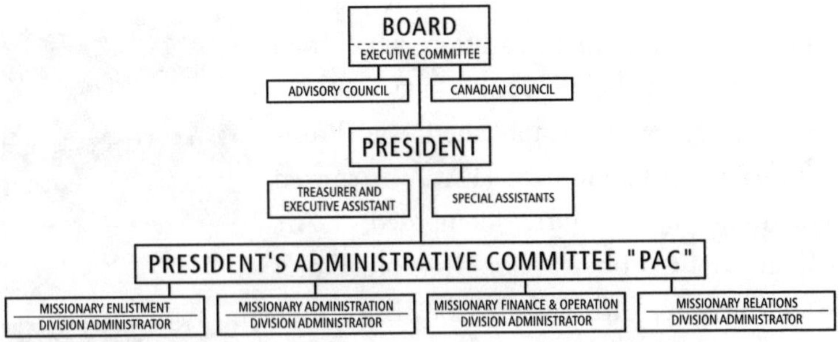

Seventeen

ABWE–North America

In April 1993 Norm Nicklas became the executive director for ABWE–USA. He developed the following purpose statement:

> ABWE–USA exists to serve independent Baptist churches by working with them to motivate, equip, deploy, and supervise an increasing number of their members as church-planting specialists to aggressively start Baptist churches among all elements of our culturally diverse society.

ABWE–USA Focuses on Four Areas:

- Locate and research cities and regions and ethnic, racial, and socioeconomic groups not being effectively evangelized by existing churches.
- Identify, enlist, and equip an increasing number of church-planting specialists to plant growing, discipling, reproducing Baptist churches.
- Establish a strong financial base among individuals, churches, and foundations to reduce the time missionaries spend on pre-field ministries and accelerate the process of church planting.
- Enlarge the number of intercessory prayer warriors to sustain and empower the missionaries as they engage the evil one in the spiritual warfare of rescuing lost people and establishing new churches.

Since its inception, ABWE–USA has seen more than 50 Baptist churches established and strengthened. (Strengthening means helping weak churches come to self-support.) Many churches have graduated to self-support status. These churches support nearly 200 missionaries. More than 50 new missionaries and pastors have come out of these churches, and they have given over $4,000,000 to ABWE missionaries and special projects. Churches have been planted among Hispanic, Laotian, and Filipino populations.

North America, however, is made up of more than just the United States. Both Canada and Mexico City have come under the purview of ABWE–North America.

CANADA

Ivor & Ruth Greenslade

Although ABWE–Canada had earlier established an office for recruiting missionaries, Canada was not opened as a mission field until 1989. Veteran missionary Ivor Green-slade, then the Canadian representative, was instrumental in the board's decision to begin active church planting in Canada. In a special report, Ivor pointed out that Canada is the largest country in the Western Hemi-sphere and the second largest in the world. It stretches 3,223 miles from east to west and 4,634 miles from near the North Pole to its southernmost point near Sandusky, Ohio.

He stated there were 25 cities with populations of 100,000 or more. Two-thirds of the people speak English and one-third speak French. Careful study of the Greenslade report convinced the ABWE board, in conjunction with the Canadian ABWE Council, to move forward with an active evangelism and church-planting ministry in Canada.

ABWE missionaries have ministered among Spanish-, Portuguese-, and English-speaking congregations in Ontario.

The province of Quebec is among the most needy mission fields in the world. Because of its proximity to the United States, people tend to overlook its spiritual darkness; yet statistics show that only about half of one per cent of the population are true believers in Jesus Christ.

In the fall of 1990, Tim and Barb Vermilyea began Wednesday evening meetings in the town of Pont-Rouge, about 20 miles west of Quebec city. A Sunday evening service was started in January 1991, and, by the following September, a morning service was added. The church met in a small basement apartment. Then in December 1998, God directed the Vermilyeas to a building in the center of town that had been a bar. After much prayer, the congregation of *Eglise Evangélique Baptiste de Pont-Rouge* decided to trust God and to transform the bar into lovely church facilities. The ABWE PACE program, along with generous gifts from churches and individuals, provided some funding, and work teams from New York and Ohio churches helped with the renovation. The church now has a permanent home, and the new location provides exciting opportunities.

MEXICO CITY

The capital of Mexico, Mexico City, is the largest city in the world and grows by nearly one million people each year. This mega-city wrestles with the problems of pollution, over-population, and a desperate economic situation.

Art Cavey, Terry Armstrong, and Norm Nicklas surveyed Mexico City in October 1986. It was well known that few missionaries stay long term in Mexico City for a variety of reasons, not the least of which is air pollution, which makes breathing extremely difficult. Negatives aside, the survey team saw great opportunities for evangelism and church planting in this predominately Roman Catholic metropolis.

The team shared their positive report with the entire ABWE family. Larry and Beverly Smith (veteran missionaries to Chile) and Paul and Susan Hardy (veteran missionaries to Spain) responded with interest. Both couples visited the city and were moved by the great need. On October 11, 1989, the board voted officially to enter Mexico City.

The Smiths and the Hardys arrived in 1990 and began working in various sections of the city. Severe respiratory problems forced the Smiths to leave Mexico City. They transferred to Canada, and among other ministries, taught at Heritage Baptist College and, Theological Seminary, then located in London, Ontario.

By 1994 the Hardys had planted their first church which started as a home Bible study. They served faithfully for five years until for health reasons they, too, had to return to the United States. Paul returns from time to time as ABWE's consultant.

Eighteen

Expansion in Europe and Africa

ENGLAND

England? Why send missionaries to England? Isn't that the homeland of William Carey, the "Father of Modern Missions"? From time to time people asked why ABWE didn't begin work in England. In March 1984, after several prospective missionaries raised the issue, ABWE authorized a survey team composed of Dr. and Mrs. William Hopewell and Dr. and Mrs. Joseph Stowell, to visit England.

At the 1984 April board meetings, the team shared their report. They pointed out that England is the fountain from which flowed culture, the English language, and, at one time, the flame of Christian witness to the English-speaking world; but the fires of biblical Christianity have now almost gone out. This decline has been accompanied by a great moral lapse, empty churches, inroads of cults, spiritism, and a revival of the ancient Druid religion. The curses of modernism, ecumenism, and formalism have taken their deadly toll.

The report went on to say, "The United States and Canada owe a great heritage to Great Britain. Now is the time to repay this debt by sending missionaries to plant Bible-believing churches with an evangelistic and missionary outreach." The *Evangelical Times* of England stated that less than three percent of the people attend church of any kind. The current scene, the survey team concluded, demanded that ABWE send church planters.

The ABWE team felt that they should make the southwest counties of Devon, Somerset, and Cornwall its areas of primary interest. In response to a strong appeal for workers, the Lord led James and Carol West to the 1985 candidate classes. They had served for many years in Spain and were qualified to head up the new team opening the ABWE work in England.

The Wests arrived in October 1985. After several months of getting acquainted with the religious scene in England and making contacts with groups of believers, they were invited to take the leadership in a small chapel located near the twin towns of Chipping Sodbury/Yate, near Bristol. The chapel was built in 1890 following months of ministry by "preacher boys" from Charles Spurgeon's Metropolitan Tabernacle in London. When the Wests began their ministry, Tyndale Baptist Chapel had been without a pastor for 66 years!

In 1986 Jack and Kitty Cribbs arrived, and within a few months were given the opportunity to work in the Morton Baptist Church, a small congregation meeting in a 152-year-old church building. Steve and Caroline Mann followed the next year, and have been instrumental in bringing the Baptist church in Pendennis, Bristol, to independent status.

UPDATE 2000 The growing team of missionaries in England continues to reach out through children's and youth ministries, friendship evangelism, literature distribution, and personal contacts with a goal of reviving dying churches and establishing new churches in areas where few biblically-based churches exist.

FRANCE

ABWE entered France because of a father and son's burden for that land. John and Gerry Weeks had served for 32 years on the French-speaking island of Martinique in the French West Indies. After successfully planting five churches and establishing a Bible institute, they returned to South Carolina to work with French-speaking people there. During this time, they became increasingly burdened for the people of France and made application to ABWE. Unknown to them, that same week, their son Timothy and his wife, Marsha, made their decision to serve as missionaries in France.

John and Tim Weeks, Will Davis, and Bill Hopewell made a survey in March 1985. They found that three cities, Paris, Lyon, and Marseilles, boast of more than one million inhabitants. They also learned that although 90% of the population of 55 million is Roman Catholic, less than 10% still practice their religion.

Muslim immigration began in the early part of the 20th century. Today, Islam is the second largest religious body in France, with 4.5 million followers.

The survey's findings led the team to concentrate their church-planting efforts in the cities of Cherbourg and Bayeux on Normandy's coast, and in the south of France in the Montpellier region.

Because the population is 99% literate, the missionaries decided that Theological Education by Extension (TEE) would be a good way to start.

The elder Weekses arrived in Cherbourg in 1986, followed by the Tim Weeks' family at the end of 1988. Dennis and Amy Toll arrived in 1989.

UPDATE 2000 Urban centers lend themselves well to the personal one-on-one method of contact, and to the small-group Bible study format that ABWE missionaries use along with other methods of evangelism. The missionaries discovered that children's Bible clubs, outreaches through sports (especially American football), and mass literature distribution through stands in open markets are effective means of reaching many with the gospel.

ITALY

For their 25th wedding anniversary, their church honored Pastor David and Rosezell Stevenson by giving them a trip to Israel. They were scheduled to go in February 1986, but because of terrorist activities the trip was canceled. A later trip to Israel and Europe was also canceled. Eventually, the Stevensons decided to travel in Europe on their own. Dave later testified, "Little did we realize that God would use that trip to lead us toward Italy. I would wake in the middle of the night and pray for Italy. We had been able to see some of the major cities of Italy, and I found myself constantly thinking about Italy and the lack of Christian workers there."

The Stevenson family applied to ABWE for missionary service. Their acceptance led to a survey of Italy. On February 1, 1988, Jesse Eaton, Ivor Greenslade, Larry Fetzer, and Dave Stevenson flew into Rome, with a view to opening the country to ABWE.

Their report stated that Italy has a population of nearly 58 million people. Ninety-two percent are Italian, and the rest come from Europe, Africa, Asia, and the Middle East. Rome is Italy's largest city with four million people. The team learned that 99% of the population is Roman Catholic, though only 5% practice their religion. Of 32,000 towns and cities, 31,000 had no evangelical witness of any kind!

At the April 1988 meeting, the ABWE board received the survey team's recommendation and voted to open the field of Italy. Further confirmation of God's leading came in the 1988 candidate class, as Peter and Lisa Brock and Jim and Lori Spoto were approved to join the Stevensons in this new venture of faith.

UPDATE 2000 ABWE's ministry in Italy is located on the western outskirts of the industrial city of Torino (Turin). This city is reputed to be Italy's main center for mysticism and the supernatural: occultism is widespread, with the number of full-time consulting magicians estimated at triple the number of Roman Catholic priests.

The ABWE team uses Bible studies, teaching English, coaching sports teams, participating in local civic groups, and distributing literature to enhance church planting in Avigliana. In March 1996, worship services began in a hotel. As the congregation grew, they realized the need for facilities of their own. People were leery of renting to a religious group (everything not Roman Catholic is considered a cult in Italy). After two years of looking and praying, the Spotos located the perfect place, in the right location, on the main street. They named it *Il Faro* (The Lighthouse), a place where young and old can come for counseling, Bible studies, and fellowship.

GERMANY

At the recommendation of the ABWE board, a survey team entered what was then the Federated Republic of Germany (West Germany) in December 1988 to determine the spiritual needs of the country and gain a sense of God's leading concerning opening Germany as a field of ABWE. The team, made up of Jesse Eaton, Ivor Greenslade, Ralph Gruenberg, and Mark Jackson spent two weeks in consultation with missionaries from various mission agencies and with German believers.

After hearing the report, the Board voted unanimously on April 11, 1989, to open West Germany as ABWE's 26th mission field.

Following the 1990 candidate class, the board approved seven individuals to the initial team to enter what would soon be a united Germany. With the disintegration of the Iron Curtain, a re-united Germany became a nation of 81.5 million people.

ABWE's church-planting efforts focus on two 50-mile-radius target areas. Rocky and Arlene Hartung arrived in 1992 and work in Kassel where the church called *Freie Baptisten Gemeinde*, Vellmar is located.

The other target area centers in Kusel, with a mother church led by Michael and Liselotte Landoll and two additional churches in formation. The work in Kusel is enhanced by co-workers from *Missionsdienst*, an indigenous German mission agency founded by the church plant in Kusel.

Ralph Gruenberg, ABWE's Country Coordinator for Germany, says, "In one sense, Germany is very religious. Church buildings and Reformation monuments dot the landscape. Public school education includes religious education classes. Over 70% of the population still claims membership in the established churches, although most limit attendance to Christmas and Easter. Everyone wants to be married and buried in the state church (Lutheran). That's tradition. A person becomes a member at birth, and pastors are civil servants paid by the government."

UPDATE 2000 A closer look, however, reveals that beneath the external "Christian" veneer, there exists a spiritual vacuum in Germany. Cynicism, empty traditionalism, materialism, naturalism, humanism, atheism, hedonism, and numerous forms of spiritism have long ago emptied churches where, to a large extent, evangelical theology and biblical authority have left the sanctuary. In this post-modern spiritual vacuum, ABWE missionaries are seeking to evangelize and establish vibrant, biblically focused churches.

The strategy of ABWE in Germany is to establish independent Baptist churches that maximize German identity and German leadership with strong interrelationships among the churches.

KENYA

Although Kenya has a history of more than 100 years of Protestant mission work, and the Bible is taught as an academic subject in high school, religious confusion reigns because of the varied teachings under the label of "Christian." Fifty-six percent of the overall population and 80% of the city residents of Nairobi claim to be Christian. But statistics show that 75% of them never attend church. The Lord used statistics such as these to influence the Russell Stockmans toward service in Kenya.

Russ and Barbara Stockman were accepted as ABWE missionaries in July 1983. Because they felt a strong burden for the country of Kenya, the board approved a survey. Rev. Powers Payton, pastor of the Haddon Heights Baptist Church, and his wife, Sally; David and Elwanda Fields, veteran missionaries from Togo; and Bill Hopewell were chosen for the survey. After hearing their report, the ABWE board met on February 7–8, 1983, and voted for Kenya to be an ABWE field.

The David Fieldses transferred from Togo to open Kenya later that year. The Fields' daughter and son-in-law, Terry and Sandy Washer, also transferred from Togo. The Stockmans joined the team the following year after completing their pre-field ministry.

Near the end of the Stockmans' first term, policy differences with ABWE precipitated the Fieldses' and Washers' resignations. With these reversals, it was good news when Dave and Doris Totman requested a transfer to Kenya from Bangladesh to cover for the Stockmans, whose furlough came due. Several other missionaries indicated interest in Kenya, as the team laid new plans for future growth.

UPDATE 2000 ABWE's church-planting work is centered in the capital city of Nairobi, a cosmopolitan city of three million people that is growing daily. The current ministry is located in an upper-middle-class area, to be used as a mother church for future expansion into other areas of the city, the countryside, and the continent.

Nineteen

Into Restricted-Access Countries

One of ABWE's 1983 ten-year goals was "to communicate the gospel in countries closed to North American missionaries by using extraordinary means without violating Christian ethics." That goal, number eleven of the 10-year plan, loomed like Mt. Everest on the horizon. Could ABWE ever have an effective missionary endeavor behind the Iron and Bamboo Curtains? This question became a matter of earnest prayer. The Lord orchestrated events that led to ABWE's limited involvement in restricted-access countries.

BURMA (MYANMAR)

In the early 1800's Adoniram Judson, the first American missionary, brought the gospel to the mysterious land of Burma. Since that time, many have come to Christ, especially from the various tribal groups living in the lush forests bordering India, China, and Thailand. In 1966 Western missionaries were forced to leave this predominantly Buddhist nation. Yet, during the past three decades, the church has experienced a steady growth as godly leaders have maintained a missionary zeal.

In connection with his visits to ABWE's Southeast Asia fields, Russ Ebersole obtained a visitor's visa for Burma. There he made contact with a Chin tribal leader named Rev. Go Za Kham. In 1974 Rev. Kham had been instrumental in leading a group of pastors and churches out of the Baptist Convention in the Chin State in Burma. He was looking for an organization with which he might associate himself for fellowship, encouragement, and possibly financial assistance.

Russ Ebersole met Rev. Go Za Kham in 1982. When Russ learned it was almost impossible for Christians to purchase Bibles and Christian literature in Burma, he wrote a report recommending that ABWE try immediately to send small packages of theological books into Rangoon. Russ also wondered about some kind of loose affiliation with this group. He wrote, "I don't know whether it would be wise to send funds directly to them but I believe we can consider this possibility in order to help in their desire to establish a solid Bible training center."

The possibility which Russ only considered, became a reality through the ABWE ministry called GAP (Global Access Partnerships). George Collins, director of GAP, visited Burma (now called Myanmar), and in 1995 established a partnership with the Faith Baptist Bible College and Seminary in the Chin State. GAP helps fund literature needs, including translation and printing, scholarships for students, and assistance to national evangelists.

CHINA

The evangelistic and church-planting ministries of the Victor Barnetts and Jaymes Morgans ended in 1949 with the rise of communism under the leadership of Mao Tse-tung. Thirty-five years after they were forced to leave, on December 27, 1985, Marjorie Barnett Miller, Jay and Dorothy Morgan, Bob Henry, Carl Brandon, and David Miller made an historic trip into China to visit the mission stations where the Barnetts and Morgans had served. Emotions ran high as the Morgans were reunited with believers they had known so many years before.

One of these was Pastor Chan who had been saved and trained in the Bible school during the early years of their ministry. During the Cultural Revolution, the Red Guards beat him, paraded him through the streets, and imprisoned him.

The ABWE visitors joined with Chinese Christians in a communion service. Marjorie wrote of that sacred occasion, "I looked in the faces of the believers and knew that as Pastor Morgan led the service our hearts were one and truly in communion with our God. It was touching to see that Pastor Chan, although very feeble, was able to raise his hands a little to give the benediction. After the communion service, three new believers came forward to say they wanted to be baptized publicly."

Even though the student demonstrations for democracy were crushed in 1989 in the Tiananmen Square massacre, the doors for discreet missionary activity opened slightly. Two ABWE missionaries, Bill Reid and Carson Fremont, began making frequent evangelistic trips to the booming seaport city of Shanghai. Bill Reid tells how this all began: "A young man in our Hong Kong church invited me to go with him to Shanghai for his sister's wedding. I reluctantly consented, not knowing it would mean an entirely new phase of my ministry with the Chinese people."

Four months after the wedding, Bill was back again in Shanghai meeting people on a one-to-one basis and sharing the gospel of Christ. In a 1989 report, Bill said, "During the last eight years I have made 42 trips to China, spending most of my time in Shanghai, but also in Wuxi, Tsingdao, Hangchou, Nanjing, and Wuhan. I continue to correspond with many of my 685 friends there."

Bill Reid was visiting some of these friends in China when he was struck by an automobile. He never regained full consciousness, and died on September 14, 1996.

Carson Fremont had already caught Bill Reid's vision. In a prayer letter in 1989, he wrote, "I have concluded that there is never a SAFE time for this ministry. If I waited for a safe time to work in China, there would never be a time when I could be humanly sure. The safety of the ministry is with the Lord!"

Bill Reid and Carson Fremont found a way into China in the late 1980's. ABWE's Global Neighbors and GAP programs continue to find ways to partner with national believers and organizations involved in evangelism and church planting. Two career ABWE missionary couples now serve in Beijing and Changshai.

CENTRAL AND EASTERN EUROPE

Between 1983 and 1989 great strides were made in achieving the goal of entering what were then called "closed countries." This was primarily due to the democratic changes that swept through Europe. The successful Solidarity Movement in Poland, the fall of the Berlin Wall in November 1989, and the demise of despotic communism in Romania set the stage for Gorbachev's *glasnost* (openness) and *perestroika* (restructuring) and other defections from hard-line communism.

ABWE missionaries who had been assigned to a rather clandestine missionary operation in 1988, now began to move freely in Romania and Hungary. The Michael Loftis and Brian Nester families had been living in Germany while ministering in Romania and Hungary on visitors' visas. Gradually, the Central and Eastern European team grew until, at the end of 1999, it had developed into a new ABWE world region with 68 career missionaries serving in seven countries.

HUNGARY

In 1983, when ABWE missionaries were praying for opportunities to minister in restricted access countries, Wendell Kempton received an invitation to preach in Hungary. His friends Paul Bubar and Chuck Cosman planned a trip to Hungary to follow up contacts they had made. He felt led of the Lord to accompany them.

The tour took the men into seven villages where they had the privilege to minister in churches and homes. In one of the homes they met Dr. Geza Kovacs, a soil scientist and a fine Christian, whose father pastored a large Baptist church in Budapest. During this ten-day trip a number of people made decisions for Christ. Wendell Kempton was impressed with the eagerness of the people to hear the Word of God. Before leaving Hungary he made plans for a future evangelistic ministry.

In November 1988 Dr. Kempton went again to Hungary. This time Rev. Dale Loftis, his three sons and a son-in-law, along with their wives, accompanied him to provide music for the meetings. Wendell Kempton later wrote, "The Loftis family and I can testify of God's wonderful grace as we ministered in Budapest. Approximately 20 people came to know Christ as Savior and Lord and about 60 believers were restored to fellowship. Pastor Kovacs said it was the greatest single ministry that he has ever experienced in his church." These trips were God's way of leading ABWE to eventually open Hungary as a mission field under the leadership of Michael Loftis and Brian Nester.

UPDATE 2000 Budapest is the headquarters for ABWE's work in Central and Eastern Europe. From the outset, ABWE's strategy has been to focus on training local Christian leaders to promote a national church-planting movement. Missionaries work closely with Hungarian partners in the areas of evangelism and discipleship. A resource and training center operates on the outskirts of Budapest to prepare workers for the spiritual harvest in Hungary.

ROMANIA

The story of ABWE's eventual entrance into this country began with a phone call in October 1985 from Dr. Josef Tson, president of the Romanian Baptist Missionary Society, to Russ Ebersole. "Would you like to preach here?" This unexpected invitation led to a plan for Russ to spend eight days in Romania.

Russ reported, "During our time in Romania we had eight meetings in five churches and shared the Word of God with several thousand believers. In Oradea we spoke in the Second Baptist Church, Europe's largest Protestant church. Over the previous ten years the number of Baptist churches in Romania had grown from 100 to 1,100, yet there were only 141 pastors for these churches! We left Romania greatly impressed that the Word of God was not bound. Rather, the Word of God was flourishing in the hearts and minds of a people who had suffered under a despotic communist system.

A little over one year later, in January 1987, Wendell Kempton, along with ABWE missionaries David and Evelyn Southwell and Michael and David Loftis and their wives, went for an eight-day ministry in Romania. The meetings began on a Sunday in the midst of a severe winter storm. Of this occasion Wendell Kempton reported, "The government had restricted the movement of cars due to a gasoline shortage. People either had to walk or come to the meetings by streetcar. On Thursday night the weather was so bad that the streetcars were shut down. However, the church was packed with people in every meeting. When I say 'packed,' I am talking about 3,000 people! The crowds grew to such proportion that the doors of the church were removed so that people outside could have a better view of what was going on inside."

The Romanian pastor estimated that at least 20 KGB officials attended the services. Anyone who made a public decision to become a Christian would immediately experience interrogation and persecution. Yet more than 125 people publicly made first-time decisions.

Russ Ebersole made another ministry visit to Romania. Russ and Wendell's trips achieved more for ABWE's future in Romania than could be imagined at the time. It was this trip that God used to burden the hearts of Michael and JoBeth Loftis to surrender their lives to serve with ABWE in this region.

On December 10, 1989, the communist government fell and President Ceausescu was caught, given a summary trial, and executed. By that time, Michael Loftis was already on the field and actually in Romania during the revolution and Ceausescu's death. The winds of democracy began to blow over Romania, opening the door for ABWE's entrance.

UPDATE 2000 ABWE's Romania team began to arrive in 1993. Their goal is to implement and nurture a church-planting movement across the country. Part of the strategy includes the development of resource and training centers in key cities. Romanian Baptist church leaders have requested North Americans to provide godly men and women, including musicians, writers, and teachers to assist in helping national leaders to expand the evangelistic movement.

Missionaries on the Romania team partner with the Second Baptist Church in Targu Mures, a city church which also works in 15 nearby village churches.

SOVIET UNION

In June 1989 Wendell Kempton, his wife, Ruth, Ivor and Ruth Greenslade, and Mary Smallenburger made a trip to Russia. Georgi Vins, former Russian prisoner and founder of Russian Gospel Ministries, played a major role in setting up their schedule. The team held meetings in Leningrad, Moscow, Orel, Kharkov, Kiev, and Minsk. In his report Dr. Kempton said, "No one knew we were coming but the Great Shepherd had prepared the way. Thank God He goes before His sheep!

"We prayed together, cried together, sang together, worshipped and fellowshipped together with believers in Russia. We experienced a bond, a unity, and a love that went beyond what we had ever experienced before. For the past 60 years Christians in the USSR have been hounded and imprisoned for the sake of the Gospel. Many we spoke with had recently been released from prison. These persecuted believers have a victorious and contagious Christian spirit. All of them look forward to the soon return of Jesus Christ."

The Kemptons left Russia with a promise to the Christian leaders that ABWE would do the following to help meet the spiritual needs in the Soviet Union:

1. Send two teams of educators (missionaries) a year while the door is open.
2. Publish one theological book annually.
3. Program and transcribe tapes covering Bible books.
4. Sponsor a Russian pastor to come to the United States for eight weeks of special training.
5. Establish a volunteer program to ship Bibles to individual addresses in Russia.

As of the writing of this book, all of this—and more—has been achieved to aid the Russian brothers and sisters in Christ.

Twenty

New and Expanding Ministries

Before moving into ABWE's history of the last decade of the 20th century, let us consider briefly several other significant programs developed before the 1990's.

Missionary Apprenticeship Program (MAP)

The Candidate Department of ABWE rather reluctantly entered into the Missionary Apprenticeship Program. Their reluctance stemmed mainly from a fear that career missionaries' time would be taken up with tourism and baby-sitting.

But when it was demonstrated that a missionary apprenticeship could be a special kind of practical missionary training and also a recruitment tool organized and executed by interested ABWE missionaries, the mission saw the potential of this brief experience in hands-on missions. The MAPer's benefit from their time on a mission field; the missionaries benefit from the work assistance they receive.

MAPer's—usually college students—raise their support and report to their sending churches much as a career missionary does. Sometimes they obtain college credit for their work. The long-range goal in the MAP program is to recruit qualified Christian young people for career missionary service.

The first MAPer was Carol Bibighaus who went on to serve for 20 years in Hong Kong and is now the director of singles ministry.

ABWE MAP'ers have served in over 20 countries. In recent candidate classes 50–60% of the appointees have had prior field experience through MAP (later called IMPACT) or similar programs.

Assistant Missionary Program (AMP)

This short-term missionary program differs from MAP in that it involves all age groups (from young people to retirees). The length of service may extend from one month to two years (and in some cases even more). Most short-termers must raise their support before going to their field of service.

Short-term missionaries fill many important slots such as teachers for missionary children, secretaries, bookkeepers, agronomists, builders, mechanics, and medical personnel.

They often save the field large sums of money by contributing their expertise. For example, missionary Larry Armstrong writes, "Kurt Sager is a contractor from New York who closes down his business from time to time to do short-term missionary work. In the two months he worked on our church in Australia, he saved the congregation $20,000 in construction costs!"

Stories of how short-term missionaries are used of God to advance the work are numerous. Statistics show that many of them go on to become career missionaries.

PACE: People Advancing Compassionate Evangelism

In 1980 during a fund-raising program for the hospital in Togo, Wendell Kempton requested Bangladesh missionary Jay Walsh, on furlough at that time, to create a program designed to bring in monthly funding for special projects. That challenge produced the PACE program. Jay suggested two meanings for PACE: "People Advancing Compassionate Evangelism" and "People Assisting Church-planters Everywhere." While both acronyms were on target, the president preferred the first. On April 4, 1980, the ABWE

THE MIDDLE YEARS

(1960–1990)

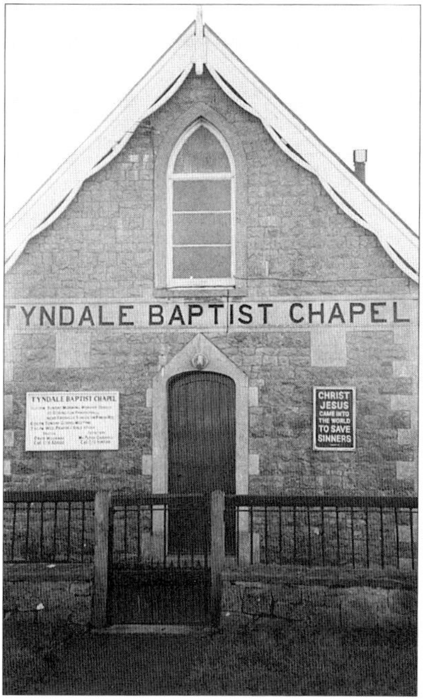

Tyndale Baptist Chapel built in 1890 near Bristol, England

Rooftop school in Hong Kong

Church planting in Papua New Guinea

Wendell Kempton, 1971

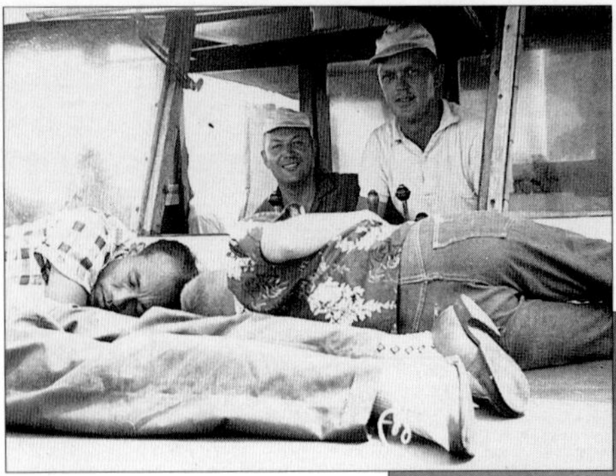

Bud DeVries (right) and Frank Jenista (left) on launch with passengers sleeping on deck

Memorial Christian Hospital, East Pakistan, 1966

Pontoon plane Hank Scheltema flew to Amazonas, Brazil

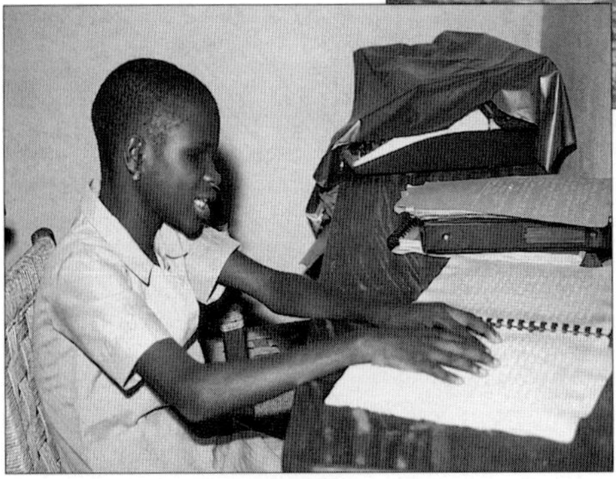

Student at the Blind Center in Togo

Left:
Church Planters opening Australia, 1974
Left to right: The Bakers, the Aagards, the Armstrongs, the Jenistas

Below Left:
Dr. John Bullock, at Memorial Christian Hospital

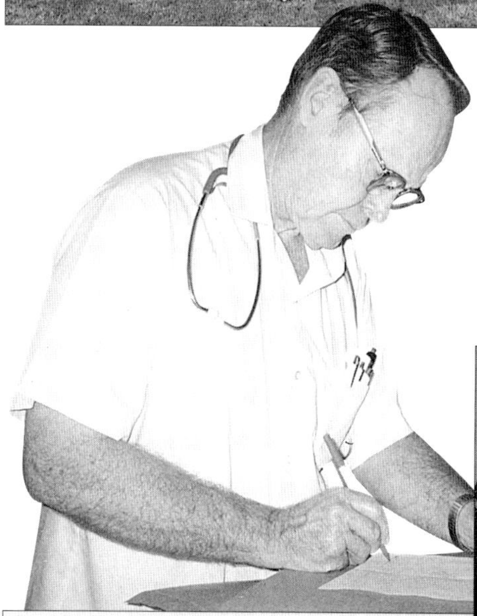

Bill Stoner in Spanish church

ABWE office, Cherry Hill, New Jersey

Left:
Jay Dyksterhouse distributing gospel literature in Chile

Below:
Harry Ambacher, China Baptist Theological College

Left:
The clinic in The Gambia

Below:
Bob Cropsey at KKMCH, in Togo

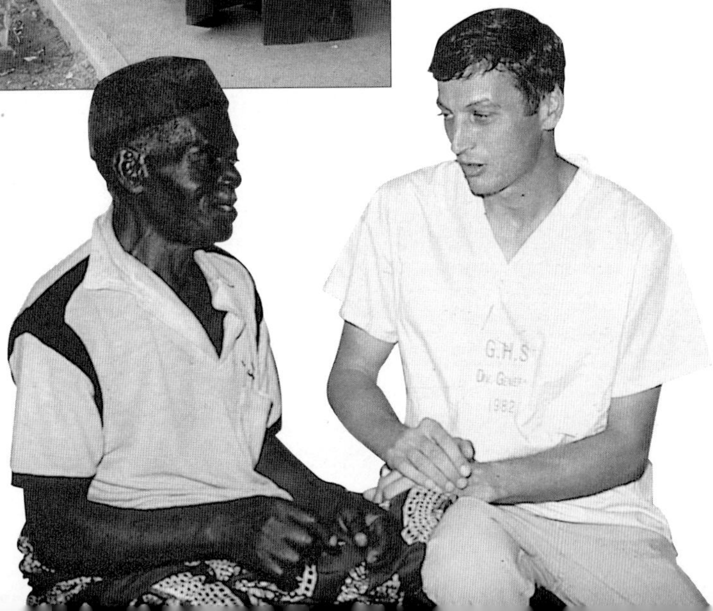

board approved the PACE program.

Jay's plan involved challenging the general public, as well as the ABWE family, to become Pacesetters for missions by pledging to contribute funds on a monthly, quarterly, or annual basis. He presented the PACE ministry for the first time at ABWE's 1980 special missionary conference in Hawaii. Thirty-two people became Pacesetters, and PACE became a reality.

Almost every ABWE field has benefited from PACE, and it is significant that approximately 80% of the Pacesetters belong to the ABWE family.

By the year 2000, PACE had received more than 1.5 million dollars to help missionaries with special needs. These include building or upgrading hospitals, clinics, missionary housing, and Bible schools; properties and facilities for camps and new churches; literature production; transportation; and costly equipment.

Ministry Enhancement Team (MET)

The MET team's primary objective is to serve the missionaries of ABWE. They do this by acting as strategic planners, analysts, resource personnel, medical advisors, counselors, coaches, networkers, trainers, researchers, and, sometimes, rebukers. This team helps field councils operate more effectively and efficiently, and assists in the areas of conflict resolution. Their goal is to have more productive missionaries, field councils, and headquarters personnel.

The MET chairman serves directly under the President's Administrative Committee. The team is comprised of consultants and specialists with a wide range of expertise.

Select Enlistees in Training Program (SET)

Bill Commons and the enlistment team launched a program for selecting enlistees (prospective missionary candidates) in training. As the enlistment team visited Bible schools, Christian colleges, and seminaries they identified men and women who had a keen interest in missions. Their names were put on ABWE's select mailing list. Periodically, one of the enlistment team members would personally encourage these students as they pursued their educational goals.

The purpose of the SET program was for prospective candidates to establish an informal relationship with ABWE. It was designed to help future missionaries build motivation and discipline, acquire appropriate academic preparation, develop skills, and obtain ministry experience. Special emphasis was placed on local church-centered personal evangelism and discipleship. The goal was to develop men and women of God who will be effective in His harvest fields.

From 1971 to 1980 ABWE accepted and appointed 376 missionaries. From 1981 to 1990 a total of 417 more missionaries joined the ABWE family. The SET program of identifying, enlisting, and following up on missionary prospects proved to be an effective recruiting tool.

Second Generation Missionaries

The 1980's saw a growth in the number of MK's (missionary kids) becoming career missionaries under ABWE. These missionaries have an advantage in that often they are bilingual and acquainted with cross-cultural customs.

While there are strengths with second-generation missionaries, there are also weaknesses, not the least of which is their easy integration into the national scene. They may tend to become more like the local people in their thinking and practice—much to the chagrin of other missionaries. But, the positives outweigh the negatives. This is underscored by the fact that more than 50 MK's serve as ABWE career missionaries.

Generation 2

This "alumni newsletter" is a medium for ABWE missionary children—of all ages—to communicate with one another. The newsletter was started by Doris Jennings in the spring of 1980 and was printed periodically until winter 1985. Mary Lou Brownell resumed the paper with the spring 1987 issue. She carried out the responsibilities until she retired in the summer of 1993. At that time, Kristen Stagg became the editor.

Kristen Stagg

Generation 2 is sent to approximately 1,500 people, which represents every current missionary family

Ministries of Mercy

ABWE builds bridges to unsaved people through compassionate evangelism. The aim is to be Christ-like toward those who are physically and spiritually destitute. That's why our missionaries seize every opportunity to minister to the deaf, the blind, the sick, and the victims of disaster.

The growth of the *deaf ministry* started in Japan with ABWE missionaries Paul and Vada Shook, whose son, Steve, was deaf. During their furlough Vada took special training to be able to teach their son adequately. After their return to Kagoshima, a Japanese deaf boy named Takeshi Minatozake accepted Christ. He eventually went to Bible school and came back to Kagoshima city to start a deaf church.

Paul stated, "God has blessed the deaf church in Japan with amazing zeal and vision. Now, in addition to the main church in Kagoshima, eleven other branch works have been started throughout Japan. The deaf have a vision for establishing 40 churches throughout Japan and sending missionaries to Southeast Asia!"

Brazil and other ABWE fields also have special ministries

among the hearing-impaired.

Years of experience ministering to the blind in Niger instilled in Dallas and Kay Washer a vision for starting a *blind center* in Togo, West Africa. The Blind Center in Kpalimé has been used of God to bring many people to Christ as well as educating and training people to live useful lives.

During the 1980's dormitories, classrooms, and administrative residences were built. New missionary personnel joined in the ministry. Blind gospel teams participated in evangelistic tours.

The Washers reported, "Our blind students were honored by the Togolese government. The Minister of Social Affairs requested that our group sing at the official opening of the International Year of the Handicapped. That event was held at the great Hall of Congress in Lomé, the capital."

ABWE continues to conduct *medical/surgical evangelism* around the world. Compassionate medical work is an effective tool, not only for helping the sick, but also for evangelism and church planting. During the 1980's ABWE established medical works in Togo, West Africa; Amazonas, Brazil; Panay, Philippines; and Ndungu Kebbeh, The Gambia.

Dr. David Clutts was involved in finding property for the *Karolyn Kempton Memorial Christian Hospital* in Togo. David wrote, "The morning after our survey team laid this matter before the Lord, the mayor of Kpalimé took us to the 32 acres the government and several local landowners had chosen to donate as hospital property. The site was the exact spot we had selected the night before!"

Dr. Jack and Sandy Sorg saw the people along the Amazon River in need of both medical attention and knowledge of the Word of God. The doctor and nurse team realized medicine can be a bridge to reach people for Christ. On September 21, 1985, over 500 people came to the dedication ceremony of the *Amazonas Baptist Hospital*. Jack later wrote, "We praise the Lord for how the hospital has been received by state and local officials and by the people themselves."

Experienced missionary doctors Link Nelson and Kenneth Cole relate how a medical outreach played a key role in evangelism in the province of Aklan in the northwest corner of Panay, Philippines. These doctors became involved because of the prayers of missionaries Chuck and Pauline Alianza, who worked with aboriginal Ati tribal people. Seeing the medical needs of the people, they prayed earnestly that a mission hospital would someday be established there. Dr. Link Nelson wrote, "God answered their prayers by supplying funds for a small hospital. The Alianzas realized that additional personnel would be needed to supervise and operate the medical work. God directed the Alianzas to contact ABWE.

The Aklan Hospital, located in Malay, Aklan, Philippines, was opened in 1982 and continues mainly under national leadership. ABWE missionary personnel keep a constant vigil and rejoice in the church that has been established. From this center, and due to the hospital contacts, preaching points give many opportunities for evangelism and follow-up.

[Dr. Link Nelson's book *With Scalpel and the Sword* records the beginnings of Aklan Hospital, as well as the other medical ministries in the Philippines. The book is available through ABWE Publishing.]

ABWE's most recent medical work is located along the Gambia River in Ndungu Kebbeh, The Gambia, home of the Wolof and Fula tribes. In the spring of 1989, people gathered from all directions for the dedication of the clinic.

A report of the dedication reads, "The official dedication was to begin at 10:30 a.m. Hours before, people began arriving on foot, by horse and mule cart, bicycle, motorcycle, and jeep. People dressed in colorful outfits were everywhere!

"Every available chair and bench was brought from nearby villages in preparation for 1,000 guests. Dr. Wayne Robilliard introduced village officials. Wendell Kempton gave a brief background of ABWE and its global ministry. He expressed his appreciation to the Gambian people as he dedicated the new facility to God's honor and glory. Dr. Mboge, director of community development for the Gambia, gave the keynote address. He conveyed his government's appreciation for ABWE's concern for the health and well-being of the Gambian people. Jesse Eaton brought a message concerning God's creation of day and night, light and darkness with a spiritual application."

Relief and Rehabilitation

During the 1980's ABWE raised hundreds of thousands of dollars for a world frequently devastated by cyclones, earthquakes, floods, and severe economic crises. Moving accounts come from Bangladesh, the Philippines, Peru, Romania, and other countries where ABWE missionaries have administered relief funds and other humanitarian aid. Acts of kindness improve ABWE's international image and enhance the main goal of evangelism and church planting.

Project Hope (Helping to Open People's Eyes)

In 1987, ABWE missionary Dan Cecil presented an idea to President Kempton. The concept was to challenge pastors and evangelists in North America to team up with an equal number of Filipino pastors in conducting evangelistic campaigns in the Philippines. Project HOPE would be a cooperative effort to reach more people for Christ in the Philippines.

In North America, Dan Gelatt, ABWE's international administrator for evangelism and church growth, planned and coordinated the first PROJECT HOPE. From February 6–20, 1990, fifty pastors and evangelists from Canada and the United States preached the gospel simultaneously all across the Philippine Islands. More than 2,000 Filipinos made first-time decisions to follow Christ! This concept of cooperative evangelism proved to be a huge success and would be used again in the future decade.

Finances

Before finishing the story of the 1980's, honor and glory must be given to our God and His people for providing the funds for ABWE's international ministries. In 1981 the ABWE gross annual income reached $8,300,000. By 1990 this had grown to over $18,000,000.

The ABWE Finance Committee, led by William Pierson, kept the annual administrative expenses of the mission under 10% of the budget. That means 90% of all income goes directly to missionary support, church planting, Bible training, linguistics, child education, communications, and ministries of compassion.

Further evidence of the Lord's provision achieved its zenith in the fall of 1986 at the completion of the Cherry Hill expansion project. The office had been expanded from 8,700 square feet to approximately 30,000 square feet. Concerning this, Wendell Kempton said, "We are sitting in the midst of a miracle. Raising funds for missionary headquarters is at the bottom of the list of priorities in our churches, and rightly so. This building is a miracle of God. We set out to build something that would facilitate the work. Let us acknowledge this is a miracle from the hand of God. We praise His Name."

Twenty One

The Big Move

The growth momentum of the 1980's accelerated even more in the 1990's. Factors contributing to this growth are many. Perhaps the greatest was the decision to relocate the mission. For 20 years ABWE operated its world evangelism and church-planting ministries from a 5.6 acres site in Cherry Hill, New Jersey. Over two decades, however, suburban development and growth had left no place to expand. The last straw: Cherry Hill township would not allow ABWE even one more parking space! The mission had outgrown the property.

In his annual report for the April 1989 board meetings, Wendell Kempton enumerated ten goals for the mission. Goal number nine was, "To develop a master plan for the ABWE property that will care for the home office growth until the year 2000 and beyond." When he said that, he was referring to the Cherry Hill property.

But questions arose during the following months that clarified his focus. The Finance Committee minutes of July 1990 recorded, "The mission is seriously considering a move of the headquarters office. This is primarily due to the high cost of living in South Jersey in the areas of car insurance, property taxes, and purchasing homes. A preliminary study has been made by the committee in the vicinity of Harrisburg, Pennsylvania, and other areas simply to compare prices."

Other factors influenced the decision to consider moving. While the future growth of the mission topped the list, several of ABWE's administrators would soon retire and their replacements would need to purchase homes. Six other mission organizations had already moved out of the region for economic reasons. Wendell Kempton shared these concerns with the board: "As we look to the future we must be sensitive to costs of operation. We are where we are today because of decisions we made 19 years ago. Good decisions must now be made so that the ABWE operation can continue 25 years from now. Our great ambition is to serve our churches and their missionaries. Our goal is to expedite this service with excellence and with the least amount of future financial obligation. Will this mean a new location? I believe it will."

From the outset, the mission leadership's sincere desire was to know the perfect will of God. Board members unanimously agreed to the principle of building a new facility debt free and without taking missionary support money from the churches. Above all, the entire team was determined to move along with a harmonious spirit.

Obtaining the Property

The board approved the formation of a Search Committee to be headed by Bill Pierson. After searching out and inspecting 23 different properties in several states, his committee selected a couple of possible sites near Harrisburg. ABWE has been an eastern-based organization. Moving to the Harrisburg area would allow the mission to keep that distinctive and at the same time permit a move to a more economical area.

The committee's attention kept focusing on a property owned by businessman Michael McKinney, and listed at $2.8 million dollars. That was a fair price considering the property contained 134.19 acres of fields and woods wrapped around a mountain with a panoramic view of the Susquehanna Valley and the city of Harrisburg. The property also included the beautiful mansion home of Mr. McKinney, a small apartment building, a five-bedroom ranch home occupied by his parents, a 10,000-square-foot storage barn, a small horse barn, nearly two miles of board fencing, and a fish pond. An important added feature was its location: only one mile from the intersection of I-76 (Pennsylvania Turnpike) and I-83, and near an international airport.

There was, however, one major problem. The beautiful property was priced far higher than the mission could afford. Initial offers of a lower price through real estate agent Robert Hughes proved unsuccessful. At this point the Search Committee asked Dr. Kempton to make a personal appeal to Mr. McKinney. At that historic meeting, bathed in prayer, the owner unexpectedly accepted the president's offer of $1.8 million dollars!

A special board meeting was called for Thursday, May 23, 1991. After the board toured the proposed property and thoroughly evaluated the pros and cons, Rev. Gerald Montgomery made the historic motion, seconded by Rev. Jack Jacobs, to purchase the property. Because of the importance of the decision, Dr. Kempton abandoned tradition and called for a written vote. After another time of prayer, Jerry Montgomery collected and counted the 19 ballots. He smiled and announced, "the vote is unanimous!" The group simultaneously burst into singing "Praise God from Whom All Blessings Flow."

The Building Project

Dr. Joseph Stowell, ABWE's longest-serving board member, wielded the golden shovel at the ground-breaking ceremony. A Building Committee was then formed to further negotiate the building plans with the local township officials. Rev. Ralph Gruenberg and wife, Evelyn, had recently joined the ABWE staff. Ralph was appointed to serve as resident engineer and manager of the building project. Jay and Eleanor Walsh, on furlough from Bangladesh, were appointed to assist the Gruenbergs as host and hostess. Jay served as project chaplain and Eleanor managed the feeding of the volunteer workers.

Wendell Kempton immediately dispatched a letter to more than 5,000 churches announcing the board's plan to build the new *ABWE International Administration and Training Center* with volunteer labor, and to build it to the glory of God free of debt. The first volunteers arrived in August 1992. Before the project was dedicated on Labor Day 1993, 1,140 volunteers from 27 states, Canada, and six foreign countries had participated in bringing the vision into reality. During the construction period the cooks prepared and served over 13,000 meals, not including morning and afternoon coffee breaks!

Dedication

Three dedication services were held. At the third and final dedication that featured Washington Redskins coach Joe Gibbs, the Lord sent in an unsolicited gift of $200,000. The "miracle on the hill" was completed debt free! The miraculous journey, covering many months of planning and hard work was over, and the face of ABWE would never be the same again.

The Miracle at Harrisburg

This property is dedicated to the glory of God and to the local churches and their missionaries with whom we labor in the worldwide proclamation of the gospel in accordance with the Great Commission. Matthew 28:19–20

We are grateful to the more than 1,140 volunteers from 27 states, Canada, Bermuda, Togo, Wales, Hungary, and the Philippines who gave sacrificially of their time and talents to construct the Administration Building and Training Center.

September 5, 1993
The Association of Baptists for World Evangelism

Wendell W. Kempton
President

Ralph E. Gruenberg
Project Engineer

In 1997 the Administration wing of the new complex was dedicated in honor of ABWE's second president, Dr. Harold T. Commons. The Missionary Finance wing was dedicated to the late Rev. Edward Bomm, former ABWE missionary and, later, Treasurer.

Moving Day

The Cherry Hill staff had been thoroughly prepared for the move from Cherry Hill that took place on September 22 and 23. The first day of official work began on September 27, 1993.

Relocating a large organization is a huge undertaking. Not only is it necessary to move the furniture but, more importantly, it means moving the staff. In reflecting on this aspect of the move, director of personnel E. C. Haskell wrote the following report:

"Big change was in store for ABWE when the move from Cherry Hill to Harrisburg was made. The first decision was to determine who would move, who would retire, and who would remain in New Jersey. Several administrators were approaching retirement age and decided they would not make the move. These included Art Cavey, executive director of South America, Mel Cuthbert, director of pre-field ministries, Mary Lou Brownell, director of the singles ministry, and Harold Amstutz, administrative consultant. Others would not be able to move because of family obligations.

"President Kempton and the transition committee had made special financial arrangements to encourage all the staff to stay with the mission until the move took place. Each of the 40 units (a single, a couple, or a family with children) who moved to Harrisburg tried to time the sale of their home and make the move without having to leave their work responsibilities.

"The day was set for the moving vans to come. Everything in the building had been coded and numbered and even color-coded for the part of the new building where the furniture would be relocated. The Cherry Hill office closed Thursday afternoon, September 23, 1993, when 18 Allied moving vans pulled up to the building. That weekend was a blur. The entire office packed up and relocated to the new facility at Harrisburg in time to open for business on Monday, September 27.

"Twenty-six new employees joined the Harrisburg staff. For two days we all met together to hear each other's testimonies. We endeavored to mold the new and the old staff into one harmonious family with a new beginning in a new place. Even though it was the same ministry, everything felt different because the building was new and we were working in a new location with many new faces. God's Holy Spirit met with us in a way we shall never forget."

A Tourist Spot

Prior to the move from Cherry Hill no one could imagine or anticipate what new dimensions ABWE's ministries would take at the new location.

Outsiders rarely visited the Cherry Hill office, but nearly 2,000 people annually visit the Harrisburg facility. They range from children on a school outing to college students considering career options to senior saints wanting to SEE what they have prayed for over the years. The influx of so many tourists brought about the need for arranging tours of the building—more than 150 each year. The scenic location, the well-appointed building (some say it is like visiting a missionary museum), and the friendly staff account for this trend. On average, 35 churches use the auditorium facilities each year for special functions. The eight motel-like guest rooms on the property provide accommodation for missionaries and others attending conferences or training sessions.

[The complete story of ABWE's move from Cherry Hill, New Jersey to New Cumberland, Pennsylvania, is documented in a book titled *Miracle Mountain, Where Volunteers Left Their Mark*, by Jay Walsh, and is available from ABWE Publishing.]

Twenty Two

Reorganizing ABWE's Corporate Structure

Early in 1990 attorneys recommended that ABWE restructure the organization. With missionary personnel serving in over 45 countries, a new corporate structure would protect ABWE in the event of difficulty in a foreign country. Restructuring would also give a clearer picture of the contribution and expense allocations related to current ministries.

With these goals in mind, corporate counsel Donald Davis and ABWE's Finance Committee formed three new corporations in addition to the current one. ABWE MINISTRIES controls ABWE INTERNATIONAL and ABWE NORTH AMERICA, which are the missionary service organizations. ABWE FOUNDATION is a related corporation to manage the planned giving, retirement, and other invested assets of ABWE.

NEW CORPORATION

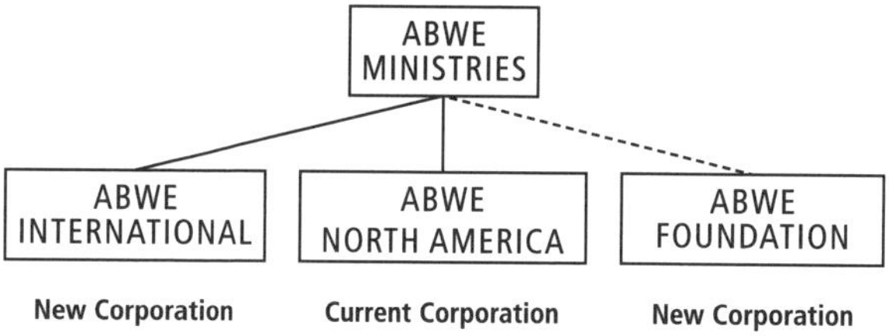

Listed below are the characteristics and functions of each of these entities:

ABWE Ministries (New Corporation)

1. The board is composed of current ABWE directors.
2. The board elects directors for ABWE International and ABWE North America.
3. Financial statements for ABWE International and North America are combined and presented under ABWE Ministries.
4. New board members of ABWE International and North America are not necessarily directors of ABWE Ministries.
5. Administrative personnel with responsibility in both ABWE International and North America are employed by ABWE ministries.
6. The ABWE North America corporation provides ABWE with space in its buildings.

ABWE International (New Corporation)

1. This corporation is the employer for non–North American ministries.
2. The board could be somewhat different than ABWE North America's board.
3. ABWE Ministries gives overall administrative direction to ABWE International activities.
4. The current ABWE Advisory Council functions under this corporation.
5. The ABWE North America corporation provides office space to ABWE International.

ABWE North America (Current Corporation)

1. This corporation is the employer for ABWE North America missionary ministries.

2. It owns the current headquarters and international training center property.
3. The board make-up may be somewhat different than ABWE International.
4. ABWE Ministries gives overall administrative direction to ABWE North America activities.

ABWE Foundation (New Corporation)

1. The initial directors were the members of the current ABWE's Finance Committee.
2. Planned Giving assets are managed by this organization.
3. Current Planned Giving agreements were transferred to the corporation on approval of the original donor and/or the appropriate court.
4. Substantial ABWE International and ABWE North America marketable assets were transferred to the ABWE Foundation for management.
5. ABWE North America provides office space for the ABWE Foundation.
6. The ABWE Foundation serves as trustee of the Retirement Trust, which provides benefits for missionary and staff retirees.
7. A minimum of one-third of ABWE Foundation directors must be chosen from among the members of the ABWE Ministries board.

Two other new ABWE entities were also incorporated in the last decade of the twentieth century:

- **GLOBAL NEIGHBORS** (GN), incorporated in 1996 to serve as a creative alternative to traditional ministry in restricted access countries.
- **WIN,** incorporated as a non-profit humanitarian organization in 1996.

ABWE is privileged to have an attorney on staff. Donald Davis, J.D., Esq., came to ABWE in August 1978 as the planned giving officer. Since 1994, he has carried the titles of corporate counsel and director of donor relations.

Donald Davis, J.D., Esq.

His work as corporate counsel involves reviewing all policies having legal significance, such as personnel, tax, and accounting policies; reviewing, and in many cases, preparing contracts involving corporations; overseeing relations with federal, state, and local governments and their agencies; preparing and/or reviewing planned giving instruments (trusts, wills, annuities) and direct estate settlements. Specifically, Don Davis has reviewed documentation of most of ABWE's foreign subsidiaries, maintained compliance with changing tax and accounting rules, and revised retirement plans to better serve and protect ABWE missionaries.

As director of donor relations, he is responsible for current giving, primarily in relation to giving for special projects and home office needs (as distinguished from missionary support); for relations with donor individuals, churches, and foundations to assure proper tax deductibility of their donations; and communication regarding their support and reporting the results. In the past five years, he has helped to raise more than one million dollars for relief projects, begun the automatic support program by which donors can direct debits to their bank accounts, and supervised the donor receipting process.

Don's assistant is Carol Moser, who in her years as a missionary in Bangladesh, was responsible for computerizing the bookkeeping system in the ABWE office in Chittagong.

Twenty Three

New Windows of Opportunity

In the last decade of the twentieth century ABWE instituted many new programs, departments, and outreach ministries.

Bibles to Russia

This program came about as a result of the Kemptons' trip to Russia in the summer of 1989. Throughout the trip to Leningrad (now St. Petersburg), Moscow, Kiev, Odessa, Latvia, Estonia, and Lithuania the Kemptons asked people how they might be of help to them. They all pleaded for the same thing—a Bible! One person said, "The Bible is the most precious thing anyone could ever own."

Ruth Kempton

From that clear call for help, Ruth Kempton inaugurated the Bibles for Russia program. To communicate the need, she wrote a book titled *Encounters in Russia*. Proceeds from the book were donated, and additional thousands of dollars were raised for the project which included not only Bibles but also Christian books translated into Russian, Sunday school materials, and containers of food and clothing. As the twentieth century came to an end, more than 500,000 Bibles and children's Bibles had been sent to the 15 republics of the former Soviet Union.

In appreciation for her work in providing Bibles, Christians in Central and Eastern Europe presented Ruth Kempton with an original ink drawing produced by Simon Andras, an artist who was persecuted for his faith in Christ during the reign of communism. The painting depicts a woman secretly copying the Bible by hand, symbolic of the many thousands of women who, in obedience to their Lord, risked life and freedom to preserve the Scriptures for their families.

Global Neighbors (GN)

This is a legally incorporated organization which serves as a creative alternative to traditional ministry in restricted-access countries. It was founded by Michael Loftis in the early 1990's, initially for service in trouble spots within the Central and Eastern European region.

At the turn of the century, Michael Loftis served as Global Neighbors' vice president for Central and Eastern Europe, and Bill Commons was vice president for the Asia-Pacific region. Global Neighbors conducts personnel work in educational, humanitarian, and business projects in restricted-access countries using these as bridges for personal evangelism and discipleship leading to the planting of house churches.

Global Access Partnerships (GAP)

Financial partnering with national Christian leaders in evangelism and church planting is a concept that became increasingly popular during the 1990's. New agencies were developed to work exclusively with local leadership. Established agencies opened subsidiaries for partnerships. George Collins presented the concept to ABWE.

George and Debra Collins began their missionary service in Bangladesh in 1981. While working among various

George & Debra Collins

tribal groups, they became convinced the best way to sustain missionary work, especially in restricted- access areas, is through training and equipping quality national leadership. In early 1993, George approached Wendell Kempton and others in ABWE about developing a ministry under ABWE auspices to provide for the support of national ministries and individuals around the world. The primary focus would be developing partnerships in an area known as the "10/40 Window," where most of the closed and restricted access nations are located.

After a year of research assessing both the need of a partnership ministry and the attitude of churches and individuals in North America about such an endeavor, George presented the program to the ABWE board in April 1994. At that meeting the board approved Global Access Partnerships, with George Collins as the international director.

From its inception Global Access Partnerships has been known as the GAP Ministry. The name is strategic because this is a ministry that stands in the *gap* in both an historical sense and a practical way. *Historically* because of the state of missions at the end of the 20th century. Today, more than 80 countries restrict the presence and ministry of foreign missionaries. That fact, plus the rapid increase of non-Western missionaries, means that North American missions would be wise to adjust their methods. *Practically* because in the days ahead strategic partnerships with godly and like-minded nationals will not be an option but an increasing necessity.

GAP has enjoyed tremendous growth because North American churches delight in developing partnerships with groups and individuals who are leading outreach and discipleship efforts in their own countries. Entering the new millennium GAP has 17 full-time missionaries in its international staff with ministries in 19 countries, including Albania, Bangladesh, Burma, Cambodia, China, Cuba, Ecuador, England, India, Jamaica, Liberia, Laos, Mexico, Nepal, Thailand, Togo, Ukraine, and Vietnam. (For security reasons several other countries cannot be listed.)

WIN

WIN is a humanitarian organization whose ministries are located in countries where unreached people groups live. WIN's secular entities provide visas allowing personnel to enter countries using their training, skills, and experience. Providing services in education, medicine, and industry gives entry to share the gospel with those who have never heard it, and leads to church planting and church growth.

Crisis Management

Due to increased terrorism in the world, and the fact that ABWE personnel living in foreign countries may be the object of terrorist attacks and are subject to being taken hostage, the ABWE administration recommended that the board designate a crisis consultant agency. Such an agency serves purely as consultant. ABWE makes all final decisions concerning people taken hostage.

In February 1994, the board voted unanimously to designate Crisis Consulting International of Ventura, California, as consultants to ABWE in crisis management and intervention.

All ABWE missionaries must sign a declaration waiver before going to their fields, indicating that they fully understand the following policy:

- ABWE will not pay ransom/extortion money or meet other demands.
- The mission will pursue all legal avenues to secure the release of hostages.
- In the event of crises, such as kidnapping and violent death, all family members are to be evacuated as soon as possible upon consultation with the regional administrator.
- All information relative to the crisis will flow through one designated person at ABWE headquarters and one designated person on the field.

- Decisions to evacuate personnel are made by the Field Council and/or the Regional Administrator.
- All victims of major traumatic events shall undergo immediate counseling and receive follow-up counseling six to 12 months later.

When necessary, a temporary task force, or crisis management team, shall be activated. At least one person from ABWE headquarters, pre-designated by the president, called the crisis manager, and one local field expert with special training, pre-designated by the MAC committee in consultation with the crisis manager, shall be included. They will be responsible for all decisions made.

International Prayer Ministry

Missionaries John and Cindy Koster served in Australia until health problems forced them to return to the United States. John was appointed as director of the prayer ministry in 1995. This service provides information and encouragement to ABWE's prayer partners. The purpose of the prayer ministry is to network missionaries with those who are praying specifically, consistently, and fervently for world evangelism.

John & Cindy Koster

John gathers information from the missionaries daily. These current prayer requests are distributed to sending and supporting churches, as well as to the entire ABWE missionary family.

With the advent of e-mail, anyone can sign on to the weekly prayer digest by e-mailing a request to abweprayer@citynet.net. ABWE's media department also provides daily information on the web site www.abwe.org.

International Volunteer Ministry

Ralph & Evelyn Gruenberg

ABWE's domestic and international volunteer ministry is an outgrowth from the highly successful building program of 1992–93, when 1,140 volunteers responded to a call for help. Ralph Gruenberg, a civil engineer and pastor who led that project, was later appointed by Wendell Kempton as the executive director of projects for ABWE. Mark Nelson, assistant to the president for special projects, works with Ralph to assist missionaries with major building programs.

These men developed a "Project Review" policy to help guide missionaries in their construction planning. Experienced professionals can often point out how missionaries can make their building project more cost-effective. Consulting and on-site review of construction projects has gone on in The Gambia, Portugal, Papua New Guinea, Bangladesh, and Chile.

The Volunteer program gives adults in local churches the opportunity to participate in a work project on ABWE's fields around the world. Depending on the project, skilled and/or unskilled workers are needed. Two options are available:

- Individual team: a person joins with other people and helps on a construction project.
- Church team: a church forms its own group of workers to go to a particular place.

By the end of 1999, Ralph had overseen 49 different construction projects undertaken by volunteers since this ministry started. This includes building churches, medical facilities, and training centers.

Pastor/Missions Interface

E. C. Haskell directs these one-day seminars that focus on various issues in missions. The seminars are usually held in a centrally located church, and pastors from a 100-mile radius are invited. Pastors interact with ABWE missionaries and office personnel. The discussion ranges from trends in missions, cost factors of missionary work, challenges of missions in the 21st century, and promoting missions in the local church. Ample opportunity is given for pastors to ask questions they may have about various facets of ABWE's missionary enterprise.

Since the Pastor/Missions Interface started in 1993, approximately 40 conferences have been held in Canada and the United States. Pastors may request a conference for their area, or ABWE may take the initiative to seek out an area church to host an Interface.

Post-Field Interpersonal Ministries (PIM)

This program was approved by the ABWE board in November 1991 as a support ministry to ABWE missionaries and staff. Bill and Ruth Large, who served in Peru for over 30 years, had previously started the group known as VIP's as a fellowship for retired ABWE missionaries. After Bill's death in 1991, Ruth continued to work with the VIP's.

Frank & Doris Jertberg

In April 1992, PIM was extended to include all ABWE career missionaries and office personnel retired from active ministry with ABWE. Frank Jertberg was appointed as the first director of the PIM program, with his wife, Doris, as associate director. The Jertbergs served with ABWE in Brazil for 39 years. PIM is made up of three different groups of people:

1. VIPs (Very Involved People): These are ABWE career missionaries or office personnel who have retired from active ABWE ministry.
2. PROs (People Reaching Out): These are missionaries who once served with ABWE, but now are in other ministries.
3. LOA (Leave Of Absence): These are career missionaries who have been granted a leave of absence from active service by the ABWE board. They will either return to active service, or move to another ministry.

In June 1998, PIM was divided into geographical regions, with directors appointed for each region. Communication is the key word in this program, and the regional directors promote PIM in the following ways:

- By maintaining a file for each former missionary containing information, pictures, and letters
- By mailing periodic informational letters including prayer requests, sending greetings and Christmas cards, and keeping in touch through e-mail
- By phoning, especially during times of illness, and/or visiting missionaries in their homes or in a hospital
- By organizing a VIP presentation at the annual Missionary Enrichment conference
- By scheduling ABWE "round up" luncheons on a regional basis

Jesse Eaton became the director of PIM, assisted by his wife, Joyce, in January 2000. The Eatons served as ABWE missionaries in Bangladesh for 17 years, and later as the executive administrator for Western Europe and Africa for 14 years.

Jesse & Joyce Eaton

International Medical Director

This is not a new position, but it took on new proportions during the 1990's. In October 1968, Dr. Warren Bibighaus became the official medical advisor for the mission and medical consultant for the candidate program. Dr. B, as he is affectionately called, served in this capacity for 20 years. He continues as board member emeritus.

Dr. Richard & Carol Stagg

Dr. Richard and Carol Stagg served in Bangladesh from 1973 until 1988, when they returned to the United States because of family considerations. Dick was practicing emergency medicine in Ohio when Dr. Kempton called in January 1992 to ask him to become the medical director. Dr. Stagg became the assistant medical director in 1992, and was appointed as international medical director in 1993. This is a volunteer position. Dr. Stagg has a full-time medical job, but arranges his schedule to be in the office one day a week. He makes good use of his phone and e-mail, communicating with missionaries around the world. He also uses vacation time to visit at least one of the ABWE hospitals every year. Included in his duties are the following:

- Evaluating and giving advice regarding the medical status and health needs of missionary candidates.
- Teaching about health issues at candidate classes and Field Preparation seminars.
- Promoting physical fitness and overall good health among the missionary family.
- Overseeing and coordinating the health needs of the missionary personnel. This includes centralizing the medical records of all missionaries on active status.

- Deciding, in consultation with the field administrator, when a missionary should be delayed in going or called back from the field because of health problems.
- Assisting in updating and developing overall strategy for medical missions.
- Consulting with medical teams on the field, giving advice and helping with supplies, staffing needs, special projects, and up-to-date medical information.

Adjunct Mission Psychologist

Over the years, various psychologists have assisted the mission in areas of testing, counseling, and teaching missionary candidates. Dr. Stanley Ballard, Dr. William Secor, and now Dr. Michael Firmin have worked in this capacity. Their delicate task helps the mission to determine whether or not a candidate should be appointed as a career missionary to a foreign field or to an alternate ministry.

Medical Missions Interface (MMI)

ABWE operates hospitals in five countries: the Philippines, Bangladesh, Togo, the Upper Amazon, and The Gambia. Doctors and nurses in other countries also conduct medical clinics.

A growing feeling of need for a forum for exchange information and problems within the medical community had been expressed. Becky Davey, who had spent over 30 years in medical work in Bangladesh, was asked to call an informal meeting of all or any medical people in attendance at the 1994 ME conference. Several nurses and two doctors met to discuss:

- the status of medical missions within ABWE;
- ways to exchange information and share expertise among medical works so that valuable information is not lost;
- possible development of continuing education tailored to the needs of the missionary medical professional; and
- a forum to bring problems unique to this discipline.

The unofficial nature of the meetings left the ideas and problems dangling, and all agreed there was a great need for a more formal organization.

In July 1996 a group of physicians, led by Dr. Robert Cropsey, missionary doctor to Togo, met at the ABWE Administration and Training Center for the first Medical Missions Interface. The medical specialties represented ranged from university professors in infectious disease, trauma, and internal medicine, to missionary physicians and surgeons from remote jungle stations. The experience level ran the gamut from interns not yet having completed their training, to medical-surgical missionaries with decades of missionary service.

ABWE has opportunities for career and short-term missionary service for physicians, nurses, physician assistants, dentists, all medical technical specialties (lab, X-ray, physical therapy), pharmacists, and hospital administrators. MMI is for people with skills in any of these specialties and anyone who was, is, or wants to be involved in medical missions with ABWE.

The conference is held each July in Harrisburg. Special speakers, practical seminars, and panel discussions make this a challenging and stimulating weekend.

When Dr. Bob Cropsey returned to Togo, Dr. Jack Sorg became the international director of medical missionary enlistment. Jack and his wife, Sandy (a nurse), served for 16 years in the Amazon Baptist Hospital along the Amazon River. Dr. Sorg conducts MMI and leads short-term trips for persons of any medical specialty, or students interested in serving Christ in either career or short-term medical missions.

Dr. Jack & Sandy Sorg

Ministry to the Disabled

Larry and Jane Golin served for 35 years in Bangladesh. Larry, a registered physical therapist, started the highly successful Limb and Brace Shop at the Memorial Christian Hospital. Technicians in the shop make an artificial limb called the Jaipur foot (after the name of the city in India where the prosthesis was developed). Patients wearing the rubber prosthesis can run, jump, and carry on normal work. Larry conceived the idea of holding "foot camps" in various locations. Participants learn how to use the prosthesis and also learn of Christ.

Larry & Jane Golin

Due to their daughter's severe health needs, the Golins had to leave Bangladesh. Larry was appointed as international director to the disabled in April 1998. He will return to Bangladesh periodically, and hopes to establish the Jaipur foot ministries in other countries where ABWE serves.

Compassion Ministries

From 1962 to 1991, Wally Stephenson was a pastor and church planter in Ontario, Canada. In 1991 Wally and Louise joined ABWE as missionaries to South Africa. On their first trip back from South Africa, in May 1993, Louise and their only daughter, Ruth, were killed in a car accident. As part of his recovery, Wally wrote a book called *Through Tears to Triumph* [available from ABWE Publishing]. The book led to his sharing in churches how God helped and comforted him through the grieving process.

In July 1996, Wally was appointed as director of compassionate ministries, which involves counseling, writing, and conducting seminars geared to help people suffering from any type of grief and loss. Wally has ministered in the United States, Canada, the

Philippines, South Africa, England, and Peru. [His pamphlets "Helping a Friend Who is Grieving," "What Grievers Can Expect," "Help and Hope to the Dying," "Questions Children Ask," "Helping Friends and Family of an Unbeliever Who Dies," and "Scriptures for Coping With Grief and Loss" are also available through ABWE Publishing.]

Wally & Jeannie Stephenson

Mobilizing Children to Serve the Lord

A missions-minded pastor is quoted as saying, "If we don't do something, THIS will be the last generation of missionaries to go out from North America." He then explained what needs to be done: "Challenge today's children."

In 1996, Jeannie Lockerbie Stephenson attended a national Children's EXPO on Missions. She was concerned that ABWE catch the vision that today's children are not only the next generation of missionaries; God can use children and needs them right NOW. Dr. Kempton said that for a long time, he had wanted to develop special ministries for children and youth, and Mobilizing Children was born.

The first *Mobilizing Children to Serve the Lord* conference was held at the ABWE headquarters in November 1998. Educators Frank and Brenda Bale, director of ABWE–Canada, joined Wally and Jeannie Stephenson and various ABWE missionaries for conferences in Canada and the United States. Plenary sessions, workshops, and hands-on involvement provide inspiration and practical help to get children excited about serving the Lord.

The seminar is vital for pastors, Sunday school teachers, Christian education directors, school teachers, home-schoolers, children's club workers, parents—anyone interested in children.

EXPEDITION

Mark & Nancy Nelson

Executive consultant Mark and Nancy Nelson developed EXPEDITION to provide high school students with a cross-cultural ministry experience and to challenge them to a practical commitment to Jesus Christ.

Mark and Nancy started in 1996, going to Arequipa, Peru, with a pilot team of four students and two leaders. That year they developed methods that would be used in the future.

Interested students begin in their home church by recruiting a mentor who helps prepare them spiritually, physically, and emotionally. Students who qualify come to the Training Center in Harrisburg for four days of intensive instruction, interaction, and a challenge to think seriously about career missionary service.

During their ten days in a foreign country, the teens have opportunities to participate in music, drama teams, visitation, and speaking to various groups. Students get to know both missionaries and national believers in their own settings. Since its inception, many young people have seen ABWE's international missionary enterprise and have gained a heartbeat for reaching people for Christ in other lands.

Pastors' Consultation on Evangelism

Larry & Jacqui Armstrong

At Wendell Kempton's urging, veteran missionary Larry Armstrong established a special conference for pastors from various cultural, educational, and ministry backgrounds to discuss the challenges facing those involved in world evangelism. The objectives of the consultation include:

- To create an environment and forum where pastors can freely express their minds and hearts, enter into serious debate, and share counsel and concerns.
- To cover the basic issues in missions today in order to assist the pastor in his leadership and personal life.
- To present instruction that will inform, encourage, and motivate the attendees.
- To listen, as a mission, to pastors, in order to increase ABWE's ability to serve local churches.

In 1997, at the first Pastors' Consultation on World Evangelism held in Harrisburg, 40 pastors gathered by special invitation. One purpose of these four days of meetings is for ABWE leaders to listen to pastors as they share their mission vision. A second purpose is to encourage them to be world mission pastors.

The consultation builds on a theology that relates the gospel to present day culture. Topics such as Developing a World Missions Church, Nurturing Your Missionaries, Islam Today, Mobilizing Children to Serve the Lord, Urban Ministry, Partnering with Nationals, and Mission Trends are discussed. All consultations are funded by special gifts outside the mission budget.

Intercultural Training Center (ITC)

The ABWE office shifted from Cherry Hill, New Jersey, to New Cumberland, Pennsylvania, in September 1993. At first, the facilities seemed spacious with plenty of room to expand. By 1997, however, it became evident that additional space would be needed, primarily to accommodate a training program.

In January 1997, Dr. Kempton said, "For quite a few years, I have been focusing our attention upon the challenge of training our missionaries. As we face the 21st century, training will become more paramount in our thinking and practice." He noted that continuing education was the norm in the business and professional world. He cited examples of missionaries returning from their first term feeling they had not been adequately prepared for service. He concluded, "Continuing education of our missionaries is the way to go. God gave us the property for this program."

Wendell Kempton keenly felt the need for ABWE missionaries to keep their skills sharp, learn how to resolve conflicts, and be exposed to new ideas and trends shaping our world in order to be as effective for Christ as possible. He realized that in the past, missionaries often went to their field of service knowing very little about the religions of the target populations such as Islam, Hinduism, and Buddhism, or the bridges that enable missionaries to be more effective in witness. Through a training program, veteran missionaries will be able to communicate these skills to the new missionary appointees.

The Mission Statement of the Intercultural Training Center (ITC) states that its purpose is to provide basic, practical field training for missionary appointees on pre-field and continuing education for veteran missionaries that will enable them to be more effective in carrying out the Great Commission mandate cross-culturally. ITC also works with churches seeking assistance in developing their global mission strategy, and serves as a mission resource center.

Robert Dyer was appointed as ITC director in April 1997. Bob comes to the position having served with his wife, Lois, as ABWE missionaries in Papua New Guinea, as the first church planter under ABWE–USA, and as the missionary chosen to open the field of Ghana for ABWE. In Ghana, the Dyers planted three churches and established the Mathetes Bible College.

Robert & Lois Dyer

Jim & Jan Ruff

In September 1999, veteran church-planter missionary in Japan, Jim Ruff, who had been the director of the seminary in Kagoshima, was chosen as the ITC associate director.

The first continuing education program for veteran missionaries was held in July 1999. The training is intensive, interactive, and participatory, with the goal that missionaries will be able to take valuable new tools for ministry back to their places of service.

The ground-breaking ceremony for the Intercultural Training Center was held on April 13, 1999, and excavation began at the end of June 1999.

Twenty Four

New Growth and New Fields

The last decade of the twentieth century saw ABWE's continued growth and expansion. Wendell Kempton challenged the ABWE family "to remain focused on our major responsibility; being confronted with the issues in Matthew 28:19–20." The president said, "This is our task. This is our mandate. This is our vision. This is our goal. This is our command. We must believe it. We must heed it. We must own it."

CENTRAL AND EASTERN EUROPE

The collapse of communism in Eastern Europe and the special trips to Hungary and Romania that Wendell Kempton and Russ Ebersole made in the late 1980's led ABWE to develop an Eastern European Ministry Team led by Michael Loftis. In their strategic planning sessions the team committed themselves to training pastors and church leaders throughout Central and Eastern Europe and the former Soviet Union. Michael explained the plan this way, "Invited by pastors from Hungary, Romania, and the Soviet Union, we focused on finding ways to enter these countries and train church leaders so as not to jeopardize either the leaders or the ministry. We moved cautiously and slowly, but our efforts received enthusiastic encouragement by Eastern European church leaders. Gradually we developed key relationships with national leaders and built a platform of credibility for long-term leadership training. We settled in for a slow, tedious effort to produce church leaders on various levels."

Two major accomplishments are now playing key roles in the fulfillment of the team's goals. The first happened in 1993 when the financial goal was met to build the *Resource/Training Center (RTC) in Budapest*. The building houses a library, resource center, multimedia room, classrooms, offices, kitchen, warehouse space, and potential space for limited dormitory facilities.

A second goal was met in 1995 when the Ukraine team dedicated the *Resource/ Training Center (RTC) in Odessa*. The center is now used to equip a new generation of church planters and to help in the development of a national church-planting movement in Ukraine.

The Michael Loftis and Brian Nester families were the first resident missionaries to move into Budapest, Hungary, in 1990. Budapest would become the center for expanding into the surrounding countries. And, expand they did! The governance of each team is directed by a country coordinator as listed below:

- Hungary was opened in 1990.
  Current country coordinator is Steve Winget.
- Ukraine was opened in 1992.
  Current country coordinator is Duane Early.
- Romania was opened in 1993.
  Current country coordinator is Doug Martin.
- Slovakia was opened in 1995.
  Current country coordinator is Donald Eade.
- Bosnia was opened in 1996.
  Current country coordinator is Mark Nikitin.

The Kosovo crisis in 1999 provided new opportunities for ministry in Kosovo and surrounding countries. The team continues to expand their circle of ministry by exploring new opportunities in Bulgaria, the Czech Republic, Crimea, and the Middle East.

UPDATE 2000 The Central and Eastern Europe team operates by the "20/20 Vision" plan. The goal is to initiate or facilitate a Baptist church-planting movement in every country in the region by the year 2020. "Initiate" means to locate totally unreached areas and begin church planting. "Facilitate" means to find an existing church where national partners request help and work with them. It takes a TEAM to carry out this vision. And because the task is so big, it takes a DREAM, that with God's help the 665 million people of Central and Eastern Europe, living in many time zones, can be reached for Christ.

THAILAND

ABWE personnel once again surveyed Thailand but, with limited opportunities to obtain resident visas, it did not seem possible for foreign missionaries to enter this land. PABWE (the Philippine Association of Baptists for World Evangelism), however, was able to enter Thailand and has done a superb job of evangelism and church planting. In 1991 a small English-speaking group of expatriates, Thai students, and missionaries were meeting in the city of Bangkok on Sunday evenings. Because this ministry showed great potential, PABWE missionaries asked ABWE's board to consider sending a missionary to develop that ministry under their umbrella and using a visa slot available to them. After discussion and prayer the board voted "to move ahead encouraging someone to go into Thailand for a short-term ministry with a view to finding someone for a permanent ministry there."

UPDATE 2000 The first ABWE career missionaries to Thailand, Don and Gail Craft, were appointed in the 1996 candidate class. They were experienced Thai-speaking missionaries having served there for 16 years. They arrived in 1998 to work beside PABWE missionaries in church planting and national leadership training. The ABWE board voted officially to open Thailand for career ABWE personnel in 1999.

Thailand's population is 95% Buddhist. Although Thais are nominally tolerant of other religions, family pressure and societal persecution make taking a stand for Christ difficult.

GHANA

In January 1992 Rev. Robert Dyer; missionaries from adjacent Togo, Tim Tucker, Dave Moody, Kay Washer, and Ron Washer; and board member Bill and Nancy Amstutz made a survey in Ghana. They targeted the Volta Region, especially the cities of Ho and Hohoe. About that survey, Bob reported, "We found a beautiful country situated along the deep blue Atlantic coast of West Africa. More important, we found the Ghanaian people to be a loving, gracious people with smiling hopeful faces—precious in the sight of God. The Ghanaian people are also well educated. English is their national language.

"We met with government officials to discuss the possibility of opening a mission field and offering education in village areas. Some humanitarian service to the people is necessary before any foreign organization can receive government approval. These officials were receptive to our proposal. Soon after our visit they granted ABWE clearance to enter the country. On April 14, 1992, the ABWE board voted unanimously to open the field of Ghana."

The survey of Ghana was unique in that the request came from the Togo field council. Missionaries and national leaders, especially at the hospital in Togo, often saw Ewe tribal people crossing back and forth across the border. They were concerned about those who lived in Ghana.

When Pastor Dyer was asked to be a part of the Ghana survey team, he had no specific interest or desire to participate in opening the field. However, when others found it impossible to go, Bob could not let the opportunity slip away. He submitted his resignation to Shawnee Baptist Church in Shamong, New Jersey, after 16 years of ministry, and applied to ABWE. At the September 1992 meetings the board voted to appoint Bob and Lois Dyer to open the new field of Ghana.

After nearly five years of pioneering the Ghana field, the Dyers turned over the work to David and Doris Totman, who transferred from Kenya. The Dyers left behind the new Mathetes Bible College (15 students), two established churches, and two churches in the formation stage.

UPDATE 2000 Jim and Carole Plunkitt, who had earlier served in Togo, transferred to Ghana from their work in Portugal in 1997. Kurt and Barbara Matthews arrived in Ghana early in 2000.

On May 22, 1999, the Mathetes Bible College (MBBC) celebrated its first graduation. The school was started to train Ghanaian men to lead churches in Ghana, but the Lord is using the school to train people to serve and rebuild ministries in other West African nations, such as Liberia, as well.

SINGAPORE

Since 1983 ABWE missionaries have been involved in Singapore with GRBSEP/ABTS (Grand Rapids Baptist Seminary Extension Program and Asian Baptist Theological Seminary). This program offers graduate-level theological education to eligible national church leaders and foreign missionaries in Asia. Resident seminars are held twice a year for two weeks in each country associated with the program. Professors travel to the various countries. This enables pastors, church leaders, Bible women, Bible college faculty, Christian school teachers, and missionaries from Europe, North America, Australia, New Zealand, Korea, the Philippines, and Hong Kong to continue their ministries as well as their education.

While government regulations preclude a ministry of personal church planting, ABWE missionaries working with GRBSEP are able to team with Singaporean ministries to help evangelize this city/state. Also, an academic policy from the main institution in Grand Rapids, Michigan, requires GRBSEP personnel to be full time in teaching (40 hours per week), and states that any other ministry must be approved by GRBSEP. In November 1992, the board voted unanimously "to open the specialized field of Singapore in accordance with the above stipulations."

UPDATE 2000 Each country has its own on-site country coordinator. Norm and Louise Barnard and Bob and Esther Howder direct the program and manage the office work generated by 200 students living in 19 different countries. Over the 15 years of its existence, 93 men and women have received master's degrees, and 40 new students in 1999 illustrate the potential of this program. Shaping the theology of Asia is the all-important task today, because the maturing Asian church will be tomorrow's leaders.

CAMBODIA

For centuries the people of Cambodia have lived in spiritual darkness. Into this climate a man arose who utterly devastated the nation. Pol Pot murdered millions of his own people and encouraged inhumanity. Starvation, misery, personal loss, and death became the companions of the masses. In four years it is estimated that over three million people were brutally killed. Seventeen years after this hell-on-earth period, ABWE administrators and a missionary team surveyed Cambodia with a view to open the country for resident missionary service.

In February and March 1995, ABWE's executive administrator for the Far East, Russ Ebersole, visited Cambodia and contacted government officials in the Religious Affairs Department. He made the initial inquiries about ABWE working in Cambodia. Other ABWE administrators also visited the country and brought back their reports. In April 1996 the board voted unanimously to approve the opening of Cambodia as a new ABWE field.

Learning of this new opportunity, in 1997 God led experienced missionaries Jim and Shirlie Moore to transfer from Singapore to pioneer the work in Phnom Penh. Within a couple of years, others joined them including Robert and Kristi Cady, Angela Atwell, and Dr. Barry and Katherine White, who transferred from Togo.

UPDATE 2000 Even during the initial period of adjustment and language study, significant strides were made in laying a foundation for ministry in Cambodia. Through Bible studies and personal contacts, groups of new believers and interested inquirers are forming. Reaching out to the thousands of street children whose lives are often in danger has won many children and their families for Christ, resulting in a growing congregation of adult believers.

MONGOLIA

Seven hundred years ago golden hordes of Mongols swept across Asia and half of Europe under the leadership of Genghis Khan. Since that time the world has been fascinated with the hardy peoples of Mongolia. With the fall of Marxist communism in the early 1990's, God opened the door for the gospel in that landlocked country.

Of Mongolia's two million inhabitants, 40% live in remote rural settings. The national government is cautiously democratic, but communists retain partial control of local politics.

ABWE personnel made two survey trips to Mongolia. The first, in October 1996, was composed of Bill Commons, Jay Walsh, Craig Kordic, and Michael Loftis. In February 1997 the board voted to open Mongolia as an ABWE field after hearing detailed reports from Bill and Jay. That July, Chris and Maura Pilet and Kerry and Wanda Yankowy were appointed to serve in Mongolia. A second fact-finding trip was made a year later in September 1997 with Bill and Sharon Commons, Jay Walsh, Jacqui Armstrong, advisory board member Donald Callan, the Pilets, and the Yankowys.

During the Pilets pre-field ministry, Maura suffered an aneurysm and died on April 26, 1998. The Yankowys had already resigned, and the opening of Mongolia seemed bleak. Chris Pilet writes, "The months following Maura's death were difficult, and the children and I struggled to discern God's direction for our lives. Ultimately His will became clear as we came to know and love Nicole, a missionary also appointed to Mongolia. Nicole and I were married in January 1999, and once again we look forward to serving the Lord in Mongolia."

Adrian and Elaine Whitlock joined the Mongolia team in 1999. ABWE's first missionaries should arrive in the capital city of Ulaan Baatar in 2000.

URUGUAY

Uruguay is one of the smallest countries of South America, with a population of approximately 3,500,000. Montevideo is the capital, with almost half of the total population. Uruguay is a secular state, purporting to believe in the separation of church and state, but more often than not political preferences favor the Roman Catholics.

David Southwell, executive administrator for South America, missionaries Ronald Self and Jim Christian, and board member Ronald Berrus made a survey of Uruguay on October 24–30, 1995.

The survey team recommended that ABWE open Uruguay as a new field of ministry. The board voted in favor of their recommendation. Since that decision, however, no one has felt challenged to pioneer this field. ABWE keeps the possibility open for the future.

MACAU

In October 1996 Bill Commons, Jay Walsh, Craig Kordic, and Gil Thomas (representing the Portugal field council) made a two-day survey of the then Portuguese Colony of Macau on the coast of China. Statistics say this country contains the least evangelized Chinese population in the world. The door is still open to Macau, although on December 19, 1999, China regained the country after 400 years of Portuguese rule.

ABWE's strategy is to target the thousands of Mandarin-speaking Chinese who have come from Beijing to govern Macau. The goal is to start house churches by teaching English as a Second Language (ESL) and other initiatives.

NEPAL

Nepal is a tiny landlocked buffer country between India and China. Eight of the world's 14 highest mountains, including Everest, are in Nepal. Only 10% of the country can be reached by road. Most places have no electricity.

Nepal is the only country in the world where Hinduism is the state religion. The hills and mountains are dotted with Hindu temples and Buddhist monasteries.

Nepal's 20 million people speak 125 languages and dialects. Many of these languages are still unwritten, so the Bible is not available. Russ and Nancy Ebersole did the first survey of Nepal in 1993. In January 1999, Jay Walsh, Donald Callan, and seminary student Barry Farlow spent a week interviewing expatriates and nationals in the cities of Kathmandu and Pokhara. ABWE is poised to enter Nepal in God's timing.

INDONESIA

Russ Ebersole, Norm Nicklas, and Larry Armstrong made a trip to Indonesia in 1993 at the invitation of the Convention of Indonesian Baptist Churches. They were impressed with the leaders and their ministry. Nothing further has been done in this regard, but the challenge remains viable for the future.

CENTRAL AMERICA AND THE CARIBBEAN

At the February 1993 board meetings Wendell Kempton requested the endorsement of the board to proceed with opening this new section of the world, which he said was "wide open to the gospel." This would involve raising up missionaries and nationals, supported by churches in North America, to do evangelism and church planting. The board voted unanimously in favor of this recommendation. Missionary to Argentina Dan Gelatt, Jr., was appointed as the executive administrator for this region.

After cancer claimed the life of his wife, Cindy, Dan resigned in 1996. Veteran missionary Larry Smith takes up the story: "I was appointed as the regional coordinator for the Caribbean and Central America in the spring of 1996. My wife, Beverly, and I had originally planned to help Dan in either the Caribbean or Central America. Now we are responsible for both areas. Bev and I had been involved in Cuba for two years prior to this assignment, so our ministry in Cuba became ABWE's entrance into that country.

"We have been invited to assist a mission in Trinidad and Tobago. Also we are working with a group of Baptist churches in Nicaragua where there are 27 independent Baptist churches and none of the pastors have had even one hour of formal training. This could result in a great opportunity to minister in that country."

Larry and Bev continue teaching in a seminary in Cuba. In 1998 they were able to administrate $85,000 given by churches in North America as relief to Nicaragua after Hurricane Mitch devastated the region.

UPDATE 2000 Paul and Patty Collier are resident missionaries in San Jose, Costa Rica. Other couples are on pre-field for Costa Rica, Cuba, and Trinidad and Tobago. Additional theologically trained individuals will find ample opportunities for ministry in Central America and the Caribbean.

Twenty Five

People and Progress

A good leader makes every effort to rally around him a team of godly men and women. He seeks to find people who combine a servant's heart with good common sense. Wendell Kempton has done that with the staff serving the ABWE missionary family. ABWE personnel come under one of four administrative divisions:

- Management and Finance
- Enlistment and Pre-field
- Mission Relations
- Missionary Administration

MANAGEMENT AND FINANCE

Bill Pierson is the treasurer of ABWE and the executive administrator of development and finance. He has directed the Management and Finance Division with wisdom and effectiveness. His superintendence has played a major role in the growth of the mission and given it direction for the new millennium.

William & Betty Pierson

The finance department is vital for the ongoing operation of any organization. Although the work may at times seem routine, without this department the entire entity would soon crumble. This department has many facets and functions in assisting missionaries, local churches, and supporters.

Missionary Finance

After 30 years of service in the missionary finance area, Bob Auffort moved to the position of assistant to the treasurer, and on January 1, 1998, Glenn Priddy became the director of missionary finance. Glenn brought new computer skills into that department, streamlining it for the new millennium. He and his department are responsible for the following areas:

Bob & Luann Auffort

Glenn & Eunice Priddy

- Managing the accounts of ABWE missionaries
- Processing and sending salary, housing, and work funds each month
- Withholding and paying quarterly taxes to the government
- Sending account and remittance statements to the missionaries
- Processing and filing Blue Cross/Blue Shield claims
- Processing missionary service requests (tithes, insurance, savings, etc.)
- Processing expense and ministry fund reports
- Establishing monthly support and set-up requirements for various fields of service
- Tracking, evaluating, and reporting on support from donors for the missionaries
- Providing ongoing services for ABWE retirees
- Providing churches and individual donors with information about missionary support needs
- Responding to hundreds of requests each month from missionaries and supporters

The following changes have recently been made in the finance department:

- Automated e-mail response to incoming requests; this eliminates expensive phone calls inquiring if the missionaries' request has been received
- A support analysis report to help missionaries track the consistency of their support
- A periodic newsletter to keep missionaries informed of new developments in the finance department
- Monthly support statements which used to be sent by regular mail are now sent by e-mail, reducing the monthly 4,700 sheets of paper to less than 400 sheets
- A special section on the ABWE Intranet site has been developed so missionaries can review policies and newsletters and fill out various request forms on-line or download the forms for printing

Spencer & Barbara Jackson

Spencer Jackson joined ABWE in 1990 as director of planned giving ministries. This position deals with money which friends of ABWE leave to the mission from their estates. The department guides individuals in maximizing what they will leave to their families, their local churches, and missions when they go to be with the Lord. Spence conducts will and estate planning seminars and gives private counseling. He also prepares *Dimensions in Giving*, a newsletter sent out twice a year to 26,000 people.

ABWE has managed trusts and provided various income programs for more than 28 years. Many friends of ABWE have included missions in their trusts and wills, thereby investing in the future of world evangelism and church planting.

Midwestern representative Richard Etner and his wife, Marge, speak to churches and groups concerning biblical stewardship.

Larry Inskeep, director of accounting, is responsible to manage the various income accounts of ABWE. During the 1990's annual income increased from $18 million to more than $31 million. To God be the glory!

Larry & Diana Inskeep

When Paul Sturgis, director of information systems, joined ABWE in 1986, ABWE was operating with an IBM System/36 that had a capacity of only 6K, and a Walvoord Software System with six attached terminals and a Daisywheel printer for letter-quality output. Paul writes, "In 1990, along with three other mission organizations, we partnered with the Complete Software Services Company of Dallas, Texas, to develop a new PC-based mission donor and accounting system to run under the PC/DOS operating system. This was successfully completed and operational in 1991.

Paul & Joan Sturgis

"When we moved to Harrisburg on September 23, 1993, only the 486 server (with 4 megabytes of memory and 4 gigabytes of disk storage) along with 22 PC workstations made the trip. By 6:00 p.m. on Saturday the 24th the system was up and running again! The computers, all wired together, continued to operate as more and more computers were added. By late 1999, the office had approximately 90 computers on the network, all of them with updated versions.

"In 1994 ABWE incorporated e-mail into the system and registered abwe.org as our exclusive address. From 1995 to 1997 Glenn Priddy helped make significant advances with his programming skills. E-mail is now pervasive within the mission family and thousands of messages daily go in and out of the system to locations around the globe. E-mail has transformed the way the mission communicates both professionally and personally.

"The Internet has become a household word and ABWE disseminates information worldwide through the website http://www.abwe.org."

Maintenance

The present building and grounds maintenance team joined the staff on a permanent basis after serving as volunteers during the building construction project. Gary Campbell, retired engineer from the John Deere Company, in Iowa, is the director of operational services. He is responsible for the maintenance of the building and grounds. Serving with Gary are David Purrington (physical plant/building and construction) and Glenn Barnhart (physical plant/grounds and equipment).

Gary & Daneen Campbell

David & Pam Purrington

Glenn & Helen Barnhart

ENLISTMENT

When Bill Commons became the executive administrator for the Far East in 1995, Don Trott was moved from co-director to the executive administrator of enlistment and pre-field ministries.

The Enlistment Department serves the local church in helping select, screen, train, and send those whom the church has set apart for missionary service. This department works in cooperation with the pastor and leadership of the local church. The local church is the sending agency; ABWE is the servicing agency. Missionary candidates appreciate the Enlistment Department's speedy response to their inquiries, and the follow-up through phone calls, correspondence, and personal visits.

Don & Ruth Trott

The following ministry opportunities are available and administered by the Enlistment Department:

- *Career missions* is the heart of the missionary endeavor. This is for those seeking to be involved in world evangelism as a lifelong career. From 1990 through 1999 the enlistment department presented 502 candidates to the ABWE board for missionary appointment. To the glory of God, and for reasons unknown to ABWE, the six years of Candidate Seminars from 1994–1999 have brought the highest total of new missionaries into the ABWE family.
- *EXPEDITION* has been developed to let high school students see cross-cultural ministry up close, and challenge them to a practical commitment to Christ.

IMPACT is ABWE's program for college-age students seeking avenues for short-term (often summer) ministry. This program replaced MAP (Missionary Apprenticeship Program). Three options are available:

- IMPACT Teams—for the individual who wants to be part of a structured team.
- IMPACT Associates—for the individual who wants to target a certain area of ministry in preparation for his future service for the Lord.
- IMPACT Internship—for the individual seeking a more intense mentorship with ABWE missionaries. This may be used for college credit at the discretion of the academic institution.

AMP (Assistant Missionary Program) provides adults opportunities to use their skills and abilities to share the gospel through service with career missionaries for periods of time from six weeks to two years. Over 200 people were involved in AMP during 1999.

In 1998–1999, approximately 400 individuals served through EXPEDITION, IMPACT, and AMP or were appointed for career service.

Pre-Field

Veteran missionary to Brazil, Mel Cuthbert, had been director of pre-field and church ministries. Upon his retirement, church ministries was transferred to the oversight of the Mission Relations Division and pre-field became part of the Enlist-ment Department.

Loren & Barbara Andersen

Previous ministry as a pastor for 25 years prepared Loren Andersen for his work with pre-field missionaries. Loren Andersen, ably assisted by his wife, Barbara, is the director of pre-field ministries. Working closely with Don Trott, Loren assists local churches in shepherding new missionaries from the time of their board appointment until they leave for language school or their field of service.

Loren explains, "In the months following the board's appointment, I visit the missionary appointees and their pastors on-site. This provides the opportunity to bond the sending church and ABWE together on behalf of the missionary. Annual return visits are made to most missionary appointees and their pastors whenever they desire." Loren's pastoral care and encouragement of the appointees has helped in getting career missionaries on their fields sooner than before.

MISSION RELATIONS

Mission Relations is the church and public relations arm of ABWE and the personnel department.

E. C. & Carolyn Haskell

Church Relations

This department communicates with more than 13,000 churches, helping them maintain a missionary emphasis and keeping them informed about current events and trends in missions.

An information piece called *Tips to Pastors* is sent to approximately 7,000 pastors every month. These are timely helps, ideas, and suggestions for promoting missions in the local church.

The church relations department conducts the *Pastors/Mission Interface*. (See chapter 23 for further information.)

Personnel

E. C. Haskell is in charge of the personnel in the Harrisburg International Administration and Training Center, a group, which at the end of 1999, consisted of 54 full-time workers, 14 part-time workers, and 9 full-time volunteers.

In addition to the volunteers who work regularly, Daneen Campbell seeks out individuals from area churches and beyond who help in a variety of ways, from cooking and cleaning, doing clerical work and stuffing envelopes, to mowing the 55 acres of grass on the compound. Volunteers provide over 20,000 hours of service per year.

The following areas also come under the Mission Relations division:

- *Compassionate Ministries* (See chapter 23 for further information.)

- *Mobilizing Children to Serve the Lord* (See chapter 23 for further information.)

Publications Department

Jeannie Lockerbie Stephenson was appointed director of publications in 1995, taking over from Ruth Trott, who served with distinction as interim director of publications from the fall of 1992. The publications department produces ABWE's official organ, *The Message*, four times a year. Kristen Stagg is the assistant editor.

Under Jeannie's leadership ABWE Publishing was started. While the mission has always printed promotional material and even some books, now the publications department produces and markets missionary biographies, accounts of missionary activities, and practical helps to show people what God is doing in missions today. The publications department has given ABWE more exposure to the general reading public, which has been a factor in the growth of the mission in recent years.

Since 1995, the following books have been produced and are available through ABWE Publishing:

- *Against All Odds*, by Jay Walsh
- *No Greater Joy*, by Ruth Woodworth
- *With Scalpel and the Sword*, by Dr. Link Nelson
- *It Could Happen to You*, by Dr. John Bullock
- *Kidnapped* (children's story), by Don and Helen Hare
- *Miracle Mountain*, by Jay Walsh
- *How Many More Barneys?* by Dan Hopkins
- *Jungle Myths*, by Keith Kaynor
- *Me? A Missionary?* by Millie Crouch
- A *Poetic Interlude*, by Millie Crouch
- *Missions in the Local Church*, compiled by Mel Cuthbert/ Jeannie Lockerbie

The publications department also acts as a service agency providing churches and individuals with literature, information, and visuals to keep people informed about missions. They provide lists of resources for missions education; serve as a resource for obtaining foreign language Bibles and Christian literature; and conduct training sessions for candidates and missionaries in areas of communication. The staff also makes available timely and topical books at special conferences and conducts writer's conferences.

Media Ministries

Wayne and Sharon Haston joined ABWE in 1995. Prior to his official ap-pointment, Wayne was invited to visit the mission and to make recommendations for moving the media department into the 21st century. After that consultation, ABWE asked him to join the staff full time as the director of ABWE Media Ministries. He, along with veteran missionary Bob Henry (35mm slide programs producer) and Mark Henry (video producer), has already made great strides towards the main goal. In 1997 Jeff Raymond joined the staff as photographer/computer graphics designer. Jeff replaced Neville Chin, who went to be with the Lord in 1996.

Wayne & Sharon Haston

Media Ministries' responsibilities include:

- Producing media presentations for pre-field and furloughing missionaries as well as for ABWE representatives and administrators
- Assisting ABWE personnel with media-related needs such as purchasing equipment, creating computer graphics, duplicating slides
- Setting up and operating media equipment used at ABWE meetings such as the ME Conference, candidate seminar, board meetings, and field preparation seminars

- Developing and maintaining the ABWE web sites. The ABWE web site http://www.abwe.org was established in 1996. Sharon Haston updates the home page daily from Monday through Friday

Bob & Pat Henry

Mark & Carol Henry

Jeff Raymond

Before 1995 the media department produced mostly 35mm slide or multimedia presentations. By 1999, the department was able to offer several options: video, overhead transparencies, powerpoint, and Scala (computer based multimedia slide presentations).

The final years of the 1990s were marked by a movement within the department in the direction of computer-based (digital) media. The addition of video production has also made it possible to create corporate video presentations for mass distribution. The department has also begun to emphasize training for missionaries and offers courses and workshops on photography, video production, and computer graphics.

The following corporate videos are available through the ABWE media department:

- *It's a Big World*
- *Lights in a Dark World*
- *Until All the World Hears*
- *From Warriors to Wanderers* (Mongolia)
- *On Wings of Love* (Aviation ministry)
- *Those in Darkness* (Blind school in Togo)

MISSIONARY ADMINISTRATION

This division oversees missionary work around the world. It is responsible for developing strategy, and encouraging teamwork, compatibility, and accountability among the missionaries, as well as for opening new fields of service. The actual operation of each part of the world in which ABWE serves is directed through local field councils or regional teams. Executive administrators serve as a bridge between the mission fields, the ABWE headquarters, and the supporting churches.

Ron & Ann Washer

At the beginning of 2000, the following *executive administrators* were responsible for the areas of the world listed below:

Michael & JoBeth Loftis

- **Africa:** Ron Washer began duties in February 2000 (after Jesse Eaton became director of post-field interpersonal ministries)
- **Central and Eastern Europe and the Middle East:** Michael Loftis
- **Western Europe:** Jack Shiflett (assumed his position on January 1, 1998, after the administration of Africa and Western Europe was divided)

Jack & Cheryl Shiflett

- **The Far East:** Bill Commons (appointed in 1995 after Russ Ebersole became vice president for missionary ministries)
- **North America:** Norman Nicklas
- **South America:** David Southwell (appointed after the retirement of Arthur Cavey in 1994)

- **Central America and the Caribbean:** Larry Smith, designated as regional coordinator

Norman & Evelyn Nicklas

Executive administrators interact with supporting churches and missionaries. Continuous correspondence, e-mail, and phone contact with missionaries keep the administrators abreast of how God is building His church in their area, as well as detecting potential problems and concerns. The administrators visit their fields frequently and report regularly to the Missionary Administrative Committee (MAC) and the ABWE board.

David & Ev Southwell

The administrators meet monthly to conduct official business, with more frequent unofficial "huddles" to seek peer counsel on urgent matters. This assures supporting churches of corporate oversight, without dictatorial control over the work on each field.

Larry & Beverly Smith

Administrators are responsible to the local churches, and pastors should feel free to contact them at any time regarding questions they have about their missionaries.

Other areas in the Missionary Administration Division:

- Singles Ministries: Carol Bibighaus was appointed director of singles ministry after Mary Lou Brownell retired in 1994.

Carol Bibighaus

- Missionary Ministries: Russ Ebersole serves as vice president.

Twenty Six

The Light Continues to Shine

As part of the celebration of Wendell Kempton's 25 years with ABWE, the media department produced a multimedia presentation which was viewed during the personnel meetings in April 1996.

The auditorium became quiet and the lights dimmed as Wendell Kempton walked to the podium. Behind him burned a single candle. After a brief pause he began, "Over 100 years ago throughout North America, candles were commonly used to diminish the darkness. People valued candles as a good source of light. Fathers read to their children by the flickering candles and families played games while gathered close to the light. The importance of an event determined whether or not a candle would be lit. People knew the light would last for only a limited time.

"Our first missionary likened his life to a burning candle that would last only so long. Dr. Raphael Thomas felt it was of utmost importance that his life shine brightly to dispel the greatest amount of spiritual darkness. Returning on furlough from the Philippines, he visited a few of his medical school classmates. He listened to them talk of boredom in their practices. They wondered if the results had been worth the struggle to gain an education and endure the long hours of work.

"After that visit Dr. Thomas weighed the lives of his classmates against the adversities, advances, and fulfillment he had experienced as a missionary doctor in the Philippines. In his journal he concluded, '*The game was worth the candle.*'

"Two thousand years ago Jesus Christ made His famous and oft-quoted statement, 'I am the light of the world.' A century and a half ago a great German writer, Johann Wolfgang Goethe, died saying, 'Light, the world needs more light.' His contemporary William Carey, challenged by the darkness, began a movement of light bearers. This 'Father of modern missions' watched the light spread throughout Asia, the Pacific Islands, and vast regions of Africa. Lights were turned on amidst the darkness through the faithful witness of thousands of missionaries."

The multimedia presentation continued. Lighted candles symbolize the time frames of ABWE's history. The *first candle* portrayed the years *1927–1945*, showing scenes from the early days in the Philippines. The *second candle* represented *1946–1971*, as the mission expanded into Europe and continued expansion into South America and Asia. The *third candle* stood for *1971 to the present*, as the mission greatly expanded around the world.

Dr. Kempton went on to say, "Everyone is in the GAME. It matters not about race, circumstances, or education. What matters is the use of your candle. Has it dispelled the spiritual darkness around you? There is seriousness and a sobriety about this game and this candle. It only has so long to burn. For that reason Charles Haddon Spurgeon wrote, 'God save us from living in comfort while sinners are sinking into hell! Be men of action. Get to work and quit yourselves like men. Our one aim is to save sinners and this we are not merely to talk about, but to effect in the power of God. Millions have never heard the name of Jesus. Shall we let them perish? Have they no claim upon us? I shall never feel that we have done our duty until we see our comrades fighting for Jesus in every land.'

"My concern in the new millennium is that we be on the offensive in world evangelism and church planting; that we be a

THE 1990'S

Norm Nicklas with church planters in Vineland, New Jersey

Michael Loftis with leaders in Central Europe

Into Mongolia

Carson Fremont with Chinese students

Millie Crouch (left) and Priscilla Bailey receive Bomm award

"Where to, Lord?" Candidate Seminar

Jeepneys brought people to the meetings. Project Hope, Philippines

Bill Pierson with Harold Commons and Edward Bomm at dedication of office wings in their honor

Paul Hardy, Mexico City

Bible translation in Bangladesh

Pre-field ministries

Above:
Volunteers at ABWE office

Pastor's consultation

Below:
Passing the baton: Russ Ebersole to Bill Commons

International Administration and Training Center, Harrisburg, Pa.

Larry Smith distributing Bible to pastor in Nicaragua

Jim and Shirlie Moore with Cambodian street children

Everglen Baptist Church, Cape Town

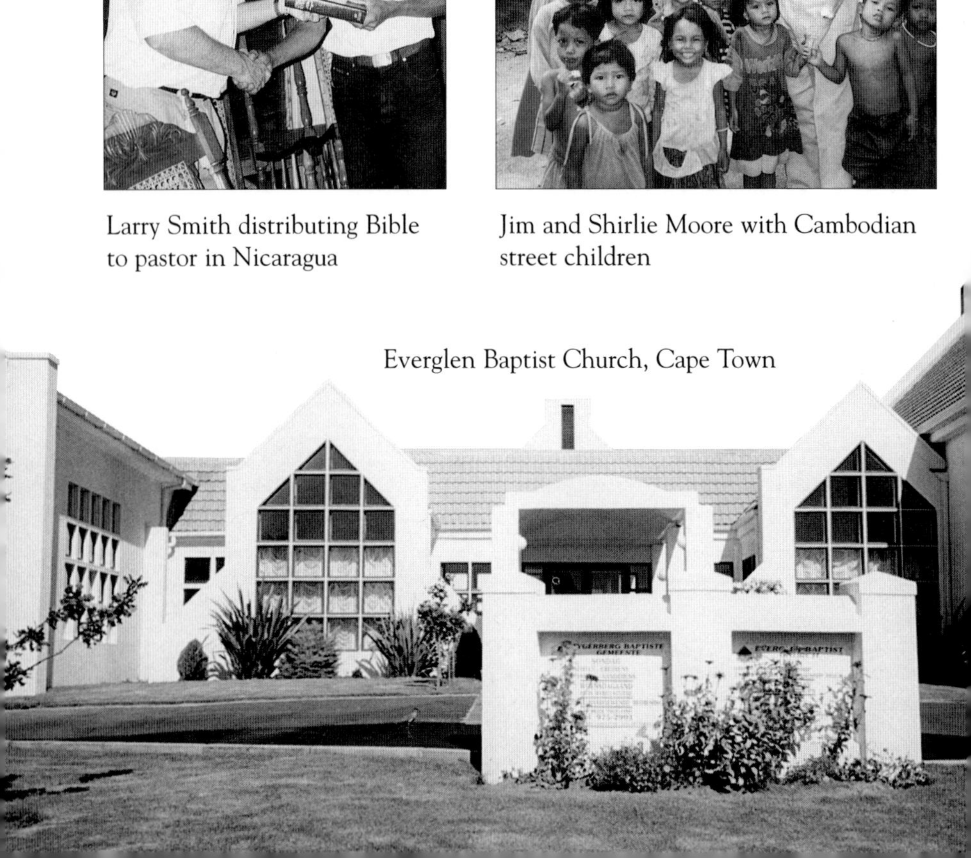

vanguard of the Great Commission. I am concerned that we be committed to God's Word by doctrinal integrity and holy living; become exceedingly proud of Jesus Christ and His message of forgiveness; constantly do the work of an evangelist; disciple with all our hearts; raise up godly national leaders and plant strong Bible-centered churches; launch into the deep where it is uncomfortable; experience an increase in our vision of God; never rest our heads upon the pillow of our achievements; and be faithful to Him and to the whole counsel of God.

"Today, missionary ranks are diminishing and church leadership is pulling back from responsibility. I believe now is the hour and the time to defy decline and to trust God for further miracles. We have an assignment. It has not changed. The task is unfinished. This is our opportunity to seize this moment of history and march valiantly forward into this millennium with a larger force for God than ever before.

"Entering this new millennium we, too, can emphatically proclaim, '*The game is worth the candle!*'

"Starting in 1927 in the Philippines with a little band of five missionaries until the present time with over 1,000 missionaries serving in 50 countries, our goal has been, and still is, to be His witnesses throughout the world, and to carry out the Great Commission of our Lord:

> *And Jesus came and spoke unto them saying, 'All power is given unto me in heaven and in earth. Go ye therefore, and teach all nations, baptizing them in the name of the Father, and of the Son, and of the Holy Ghost: Teaching them to observe all things whatsoever I have commanded you: and, lo, I am with you alway, even unto the end of the world.'"* (Matthew 28:18–20)

Twenty Seven

The Three Presidents

A major influence on ABWE's "legacy of commitment and growth" involves its leadership. In a world where change is a constant, the fact that ABWE was led by just three presidents from 1927 through 2000 is remarkable. This chapter highlights the lives of those three people.

Lucy Peabody (1861–1949)

Mrs. Lucy Peabody served as a missionary among Telugu speakers in India. Her first husband, Norman Waterbury, died in 1886 while they were in India, leaving her with two small children. She returned to the United States, where she became a teacher, writer, editor, and gifted public speaker. She rose to considerable prominence in the Northern Baptist Convention and served as secretary of the Women's Baptist Foreign Mission Society for 18 years.

In 1904 she married a successful businessman, Henry Wayland Peabody. For the rest of her life she lived in Beverly, Massachusetts, using her talents and financial means to help many worthy causes.

From ABWE's standpoint, her most notable achievement was her courageous fight against the inroads of liberal theology within the ranks of the Northern Baptist Convention. She believed the Bible with all her heart and stood valiantly for the fundamentals of the faith. She refused to be party to the inclusive policy which was officially adopted by the Northern Baptist Convention. That policy was designed to make room on the same mission field for missionaries adhering to various shades of belief. Specifically, she took up the battle against the operation of this inclusive policy in the Philippine Islands where her son-in-law and daughter, Dr. Raphael and Norma Thomas, worked as missionaries. The Foreign Board of the Convention imposed restrictions upon Dr. Thomas' evangelistic activities in favor of purely medical work in the hospital at Iloilo and gave other evidences of favoring more liberal programs. When she realized what was happening, Mrs. Peabody took the issue to the floor of the Northern Baptist Convention and led a plea for a return to biblical faith and practice, and for a thorough study of the actual situation in the Philippines.

Failing to accomplish this objective, and with an indomitable spirit, Mrs. Peabody took her historic walk and resigned from every office within the Convention. She then gave her full support to the courageous little group of missionaries in the Philippines who resigned over these issues. In August 1927, on the porch of the summer cottage of Marguerite Doane at Watch Hill, Rhode Island, Mrs. Peabody helped launch an adventure of faith in the Philippines and form a new independent Baptist mission agency (incorporated under the name Association of Baptists for Evangelism in the Orient.) Mrs. Peabody was elected as the first president of the mission, and served in that capacity for seven years.

Harold Taber Commons

Harold T. Commons came from an ecumenical background. His father started as a Quaker preacher in New England, became a Congregational minister, and eventually espoused a Unitarian theology. Consequently, the boy never heard the gospel of Christ during his formative years. In 1923 he entered Williams College in Williamstown, Massachusetts. During his sophomore year, Harold spent Easter vacation with an uncle who was an earnest Christian and knew his Bible well. The older man showed young Harold passages dealing with salvation and the need for personal faith in Jesus Christ. Harold immediately accepted Christ as his personal Savior.

Returning to Williams College, Harold became active in the Student Volunteer Movement with the desire to become a missionary in Africa. At that same time he met Miss Corinth Tracy, who eventually became his wife. In order to acquire more theological training, he entered Princeton Theological Seminary in 1927. During his second year, the Fundamentalist–Modernist controversy in the Presbyterian denomination came to a head, and several noted conservative professors were either dropped or resigned from the faculty. Harold decided he could not conscientiously return for his final year. The faculty who left Princeton started Westminster Theological Seminary in Philadelphia, where Harold Commons spent his final year and was a member of the first graduating class.

By the time he graduated, his perspective on ministry had shifted. He was still vitally concerned with foreign missions, but realized that the cause of missions was irrevocably tied to the churches. The make-up of the missionary force is a cross-section of local churches in the homelands. He decided he could best serve evangelical Christianity on the mission field by doing what he could to stem the tide of liberalism in the churches at home. The Commonses had become Baptists while in seminary and joined Spruce Street Baptist Church, in Philadelphia. They were baptized, and Harold Commons was ordained there. In July 1930, he became pastor of the First Baptist Church in Atlantic City.

Harold Commons' relationship to ABWE began in 1931 through his friendship with David Otis Fuller, an ABWE board member. Mr. Commons attended several board meetings by special invitation, and since the regular secretary was rarely able to attend the meetings, Mrs. Peabody asked Harold if he would attend regularly and take minutes. She explained there was no room for him on the board at the time because the roster was full. The Executive Committee agreed that someone who was with them in interest and spirit could attend the meetings and serve as secretary. From that time on, Harold Commons became an active participant in the mission. He handled much of the official correspondence between headquarters and the missionaries.

In 1933, he moved to Johnson City, New York, to serve as pastor of the First Baptist Church and president of the Baptist Bible Seminary located there. His relationship with ABWE continued, and he was elected as a board member and vice president in October 1934. At the April 1935 board meeting, Mrs. Peabody resigned and Harold Commons was elected president.

Dr. Harold Commons guided ABWE through many difficult years, including the Great Depression and World War II. When he assumed the office of president, ABWE had 18 missionaries working in the Philippines only. By 1971, when he retired, 350 missionaries served in 11 countries. God blessed his able leadership for 36 years.

Now in his 94th year, Dr. Harold Commons lives in Philadelphia. He is the father of four children, Corinth ("Sunny"), Elizabeth ("Liz"), Bill, and Hal, Jr., and nine living grandchildren.

Wendell Walker Kempton

Wendell Kempton was born in Iowa and saved in Des Moines when he was 19. At that time, he was a baseball player preparing for the major leagues. Under the advice of his pastor and spiritual mentor, Rev. Gene Swim, he attended Moody Bible Institute.

While at Moody, Wendell met Karolyn. She was born in Galantia, Kansas, and later moved to Amarillo, Texas. At the age of 16, a neighbor led her to faith in Christ. Wendell and Karolyn were married in 1955, and over time became the parents of Mark, Stan, and Wendy.

Wendell Kempton received further training at Baptist Bible

Seminary and Dallas Theological Seminary and taught at Baptist Bible College in Clarks Summit, Pennsylvania.

In addition to earning Th.B. and Th.M. degrees, he did graduate work at Syracuse University and received an honorary Doctor of Divinity from Grand Rapids Baptist College and Seminary. He was chosen as Baptist Bible College's Alumnus of the Year in 1974 and was nominated as Outstanding Young Man of America in 1967.

Dr. Kempton came to ABWE in 1971 from Baptist Bible Seminary, bringing ten years of experience as director of public relations and other faculty positions. His responsibilities at ABWE centered around the overall administration, fund-raising for missionary projects, and traveling and speaking in every continent. He represented the mission in local churches, colleges, and seminaries throughout North America, challenging people to dedicate their lives to God for missionary service.

In December 1980, while Dr. Kempton was conducting meetings in Michigan, Karolyn suffered a massive brain aneurysm and died on December 20.

Subsequently, God led Ruth into Dr. Kempton's life. Ruth was raised in southern Pennsylvania and earned a Master of Science in physical education from the University of Maryland. She taught for 25 years at the elementary, high school, and college levels. She is the recipient of the 1995 Distinguished Alumna Award from West Chester University in Pennsylvania. Ruth was married to the well-known football coach Lee "Rock" Royer, who was killed in a plane crash in 1973. She is the mother of Jennifer, Amy, and Tim. She has lectured on Christian education at national conventions and is a frequent speaker at women's retreats and church functions. Wendell and Ruth were married on August 1, 1982.

The Kemptons take every opportunity to share their faith. They hold regular neighborhood Bible studies, and, as time permits, he speaks to various professional sports franchises, including teams that played in three Super Bowls and a World Series.

The 29 years of his leadership have been a period of tremendous growth, both in the number of missionaries serving with ABWE and in expansion into numerous countries of the world. New avenues of ministry and opportunity have been pursued. Under Dr. Kempton's leadership, ABWE made its move from the greater Philadelphia area to Harrisburg in 1993. By the year 2000, ABWE had nearly 1,000 missionaries involved in ministries in North America and more than 50 countries around the world.

UPDATE 2000 On September 10, 1997, Dr. Kempton's 65th birthday, he announced to the ABWE board his intention to step down from the presidency in the year 2000. He named the following men as a Search Committee to locate the next president:

- *Chairman:* Rev. Will Davis (vice president of ABWE, and in pastoral ministries at Berean Baptist Church, Portage, Mich.)
- Rev. Gerald Montgomery (34 years of service on ABWE board, pastor of First Baptist Church, Willingboro, N.J.)
- Rev. Melvin Beals (20 years as a missionary in Bangladesh, on ABWE advisory board, pastor of First Baptist Church, Woodland, Calif.)
- Rev. Richard Christen (30 years on ABWE board, pastor of First Baptist Church, Hemet, Calif.)
- Rev. Ernie Brubaker (member of the ABWE Canadian Council, on ABWE advisory board, pastor of Crestwicke Baptist Church, Guelph, Ontario)
- Dr. Steven Euler (served since 1989 on the advisory board and the full ABWE board, pastor of Grace Baptist Church, Chattanooga, Tenn.)
- Rev. Ron Berrus (served since 1994 on the advisory board and the full ABWE board, pastor of First Baptist Church, Bellefonte, Pa.)

On Tuesday, February 1, 2000, the staff of the ABWE International Headquarters and Training Center met as Vice President

Will Davis explained the process the Search Committee followed; and then read the official release:

> The Vice President of ABWE and Chairman of the Search Committee, Rev. Will M. Davis, representing the official Board of ABWE, is happy to announce the fourth president in the history of ABWE, ***Dr. Michael G. Loftis.***
>
> Following a two-year search process, the ABWE Board extended a unanimous call to Dr. Loftis, and he has accepted that call. Michael Loftis will assume his official role as president-elect on September 1, 2000, and will become the official successor of Wendell W. Kempton on March 1, 2001.
>
> Dr. Loftis has served as ABWE Executive Administrator for Central and Eastern Europe for the past 12 years. The Loftis family presently resides in Budapest, Hungary.

Left to right: Michael & JoBeth Loftis, Will Davis, and Ruth & Wendell Kempton.

Dr. Kempton responded by saying, "It is a great honor and privilege for me to strongly confirm the unanimous decision of the ABWE board and to introduce Michael G. Loftis as the next president of ABWE. Ruth and I highly esteem the work God has done through Michael and JoBeth during their 12 years of service with ABWE in Central and Eastern Europe. We anticipate God's richest blessings on the Loftises as they lead ABWE in the new millennium."

As the news flashed electronically to ABWE missionaries around the world, the group in the worship chapel sang, "To God be the glory, GREAT THINGS HE HATH DONE."

APPENDIX ONE

MISSION STATEMENT

of the

Association of Baptists for World Evangelism

ABWE exists for the primary purpose of serving local independent Baptist churches by facilitating and coordinating the ministries of their missionaries, all in a spirit of partnership and cooperation.

The mission also exists to serve its constituency in auxiliary ways.

APPENDIX TWO

STATEMENT OF VALUES

ABWE is determined, under God, to be a spiritually empowered family of servants committed to glorifying Him. We will follow Christ's command to preach the gospel throughout the world. As representatives of our sending churches, we boldly evangelize, disciple, train leadership, and establish reproducing Baptist churches in agreement with our doctrinal statement. We are committed to integrity, excellence, compassion and accountability until our Lord returns.

ABWE is committed to fulfill our organizational purpose, to prioritize our responsibilities, and to live holy lives. We will not turn back from the ministry, compromise our faith, or waiver in our commitment.

Integrity

ABWE is committed to Biblical integrity. This will govern every facet of our ministry. We will encourage one another to accurate and open communication, a lifestyle above reproach, responsible fiscal stewardship, and the avoidance of exaggeration, misrepresentation, deception, or breach of ethics.

Excellence

ABWE is committed to rise above mediocrity and pursue excellence by individually and corporately improving our skills in order to enhance mission morale, maintain the respect of our constituency, and enlist high-quality personnel.

Compassion

ABWE is committed to ministries of compassion in evangelism and church planting, using methods that are culturally appropriate and effective.

Accountability

ABWE is committed to require accountability by consistently evaluating attitudes, relationships, and the effective performance of goals.

APPENDIX THREE

OUR PLEDGE TO CHURCHES

1. We are committed to scriptural integrity and to doctrinal purity as expressed in the ABWE Statement of Faith.
2. We are committed to obeying the Great Commission and assuming all the responsibilities connected with this command.
3. We are committed to exercising the spirit of Christ in our dealings with churches, missionaries, donors, and critics.
4. We are committed to the priority of the local New Testament church and its leadership, pastors, and deacons.
5. We are committed to providing faithful service for the local churches as they send out their missionaries.
6. We are committed to the principle of accountability among the mission, missionaries, and supporting churches.
7. We are committed, in concert with our sending churches, to maintaining high standards for all ABWE personnel.
8. We are committed to the principle of a Christ-like attitude in living out the Christian life before all people at home and abroad.
9. We are committed to the New Testament principle and practice of evangelism, discipling, and planting Baptist churches capable of reproducing other churches.
10. We are committed to a program of church planting that has national leadership, ownership, and stewardship in view from its inception.
11. We are committed to a fiscal responsibility in serving our supporting churches and missionaries.
12. We pledge ourselves to do all we can to bring people to Christ throughout the world, maintaining a biblical perspective and balance regarding our involvement in church planting and ministries of compassion.

APPENDIX FOUR

OUR COMMITMENT TO OUR SUPPORTERS

We consider our supporters as partners in the gospel ministry. Our vision and values cause us to recognize our accountability to God and to our supporters for our stewardship of their investment in this work. Because of this commitment we:

1. Operate under the authority of an independent board of directors, made up of pastors and other spiritual leaders;
2. Honor the designations of our partners, consistent with board policy and revenue laws, carefully accounting for all gifts from time of receipt until designated use;
3. Prepare financial statements for annual audit by an independent auditing firm;
4. Maintain confidentiality of all donor records, including the identity of our partners.

APPENDIX FIVE

ABWE STATISTICAL INFORMATION

Prepared by Missions Relations Department, January, 2000

Missionaries	**989**
Career Missionaries	897
Short-Term Missionaries	71
On Leave of Absence	10
Representatives	11
Retired Missionaries	**113**
USA/Canada Support Team	**182**
Total ABWE Family	**1,284**

COUNTRIES WHERE ABWE SERVES

Listed by region with the count of the currently active missionaries.

Far East

Australia	13
Bangladesh	56
Cambodia	8
China	4
Hong Kong	8
India	2
Japan	15
Mongolia	4
Nepal	0
Papua New Guinea	21
Philippines	43
Singapore	6
Thailand	2
Vietnam	2

North America

Canada	4
Mexico	4
USA	40

Western Europe

England	13
France	6
Germany	7
Italy	14
Norway	8
Portugal	27
Spain	16

Africa

Ghana	12
Kenya	2
South Africa	40
The Gambia	16
Togo	44

Central and Eastern Europe

Bosnia	1
Hungary	30
Kosovo	0
Romania	9
Slovakia	15
Ukraine	20

Middle East

Jordan	1

South America

Argentina	9
Brazil	102
Chile	30
Colombia	16
Paraguay	15
Peru	49
Uruguay	0

Central America & Caribbean

Costa Rica	5
Cuba	4
Nicaragua	4
Trinidad and Tobago	2

FIELD COUNCILS

Far East (12)

Australia "Field Team"
Bangladesh (2 sub-councils)
Cambodia "FCIF"
China "Field Team"
Hong Kong
Japan (2 sub-councils)
Mongolia "Field Team"
Papua New Guinea
Philippines (5 sub-councils)
Singapore "Field Team"
Thailand "FCIF"

Africa (6)

Ghana
Kenya
South Africa, Cape
South Africa, Durban
The Gambia
Togo

Alternative Field Governance

Central America/Caribbean
Central and Eastern Europe/ Middle East
Germany

Western Europe (6)

England
France
Italy
Norway
Portugal
Spain

South America (13)

Argentina
Amazonas, Brazil
Bahia, Brazil
Central Brazil
Northeast Brazil
Pernambuco, Brazil
São Paulo, Brazil
South Brazil
Chile
Colombia
Paraguay
Coastal Peru
Upper Amazon Peru

ADDITIONAL STATISTICS OF NOTE

- 13,170 churches are on the ABWE mailing list.
- Over 150,000 names are on the mailing list.
- Over 6,000 churches support ABWE ministries on a monthly basis.
- Over 1,000,000 pieces of mail are received and dispatched every month.
- ABWE's *Message* magazine circulation averages 120,000 copies per issue.
- Income for ABWE ministries exceeds $30,000,000 annually.
- Nearly 5,000 people visit ABWE headquarters annually.
- ABWE missionaries have had the privilege of having a part in planting over 2,000 indigenous churches, establishing 27 educational training centers, 8 medical facilities, and an international aviation program.

APPENDIX SIX

RECIPIENTS of The Edward and Marian Bomm Award

THE EDWARD AND MARIAN BOMM AWARD

In Recognition of Exceptional Servanthood
with ABWE since (date)
This award is fittingly presented to

(RECIPIENT'S NAME)

whose ministry consistently exemplified servanthood.
His/hers was the spirit of the Apostle Paul by
giving not only the gospel of God but his/her own
soul as he/she manifested genuine love for people
and met their needs.

1 Thessalonians 2:8

The Following Awards have been given:

1986

Warren Bibighaus—Medical Consultant
Edward and Marian Bomm—Philippines, Treasurer, Administrator
Elsie Miller—Secretary to Presidents
Jaymes and Dorothy Morgan—China, Japan, Philippines, Hong Kong
Mary Russell—Philippines

1987

Al and Ruth Conant—Philippines
Don and Helen Hare—Brazil
Lindsey and Jean Harrell—Amazon Brazil
Edna Hull—Amazon Peru
Helen Paige—Peru

1988

Carson Fremont—Philippines, Hong Kong, China
Bill and Ruth Large—Amazon Peru
Frona Mattox—Brazil
Dr. Link and Lenore Nelson—Philippines
Paul and Vada Shook—Japan

1989

Priscilla Baily—Philippines
Robert and Elaine Banning—Philippines
Art and Joyce Cavey—Brazil, Administrator for South America
Mildred Crouch—Philippines
Mel and Romilda Cuthbert —Brazil, Director of Pre-Field and Church Ministries
Russ Ebersole—Philippines, Administrator Far East, VP Missionary Ministries
Ivor and Ruth Greenslade—Amazon Peru, Argentina
Daniel and Lauretta Holden—Philippines
Frank and Sophie Jenista—China, Hong Kong, Philippines, Australia, PNG
John and Fran Schlener—Amazon Brazil
Paul and Jessie Schlener—Amazon Brazil
Ruth Warner—Hong Kong

1990

Frank and Doris Jertberg—Brazil, Director of PIM
Ron and Gladys Meznar—Brazil

1991

Mary Lou Brownell—Bangladesh, Director of Singles Ministries
Ella Grover—Philippines
Gene and Elizabeth Gurganus—Bangladesh, Representative
George and Norma Haberer—Papua New Guinea
Joyce Hatch—Brazil
Stan and Jean Holman—Philippines
Mona Kemery—Philippines
Dale and Marsha Payne—Brazil

1992

Don and Vivian Bond—Upper Amazon Peru

1994

Larry and Jacqui Armstrong—Philippines, Australia, Missionary-at-large
Darline Fremont—Philippines, Hong Kong, China
Charles and Thelma Runyon—Philippines
Jay and Eleanor Walsh—Bangladesh, PACE, Special Assistant to President

1995

Jackson and Thelma Moore—Brazil
Chuck and Caroline Porter—Amazon Peru
Don and Polly Taber—Philippines
David Toro—Chile, Australia, USA
Francais Weddle—Amazon Peru

1996

William and Thes Branda—Brazil
Nancy Goehring Ebersole—Bangladesh, Philippines
Jeannie Lockerbie Stephenson—Bangladesh, Director of Publications
Dr. Viggo and Joan Olsen—Bangladesh, Islamic Consultant

Fred and Rachel Patton—Amazon Peru
Benjamin and Pauline Peterson—Brazil

1997

Bonnie Abbas—Chile
Robert and Barbara Adolph—Bangladesh
Sandra Lyons—Amazon Peru, Corporate Finance Assistant
Hank and Ruth Scheltema—Brazil, Director of Aviation Ministries
William and Rosie Stoner—Chile, Spain
Raydene Taylor—Philippines

1998

Addie Cook—Brazil
Larry and Jane Golin—Bangladesh, Director of Ministries to Disabled
Agnes Haik—Brazil
Richard and Betty Sterkenburg—Brazil
George and Lillian Toensfeldt—Philippines

1999

Rebecca Davey—Bangladesh
Rich and Dee Donaldson Sr.—Amazon Peru
Nancy Payton—Philippines, USA
Bob and Margaret Paswaters—Hong Kong

INDEX